UNBUSY

HOW TO LEVERAGE THE PHYSICS OF FLOW TO ACCOMPLISH MORE OF WHAT TRULY MATTERS AND FEEL LESS BUSY AT THE SAME TIME.

ANDY DRAGT

Copyright © 2019 by Andy Dragt

All rights reserved.

No part of this book may be reproduced in any form or by any electronic or mechanical means, including information storage and retrieval systems, without written permission from the author, except for the use of brief quotations in a book review.

ISBN: 978-1-7334912-0-4

For Gina, Haeli, and Maya who ALWAYS have my back; always.

DOWNLOAD THE AUDIOBOOK FREE

READ THIS FIRST

Just to say thanks for buying my book, I would like to give you the Audiobook version 100% FREE!

TO DOWNLOAD GO TO:

http://andydragt.com/unbusy-audiobook

1

THE UNBUSY LIFE

What would you give to feel less busy?

Most of us live fragmented lives, running from commitment to commitment and filling the fleeting moments in between with distractions, partially completed tasks, and casual entertainment. Our lives feel like a tug of war between what the world expects of us, and our dreams for a life full of meaning and purpose. There doesn't seem to be time for everything we want to do. Nearly everyone I survey ends their days feeling like they didn't accomplish everything they intended. No one likes to disappoint or let others down, so it's our dreams and priorities that get shoved to the back-burner. Since we carry around this constant sense that there are things left undone, we always *feel* busy.

It doesn't have to be this way.

It's possible to live an *unbusy* life full of purpose and still accomplish *more* of what truly matters to you. It will not be easy, but I bet you knew that already. Together we can design a life in which you keep the commitments that matter most, accomplish the big goals you have in life and feel less busy all at the same time. I know this because I've done it. I know it's possible for you too because I've helped hundreds of leaders do the same thing. Over the last several years, I've developed a language and a toolset inspired by the natural world around us and rooted in the science of physics. These tools have proven helpful consistently over time. They have been a guide for those willing to do the work necessary to design and live an unbusy life.

I'm thrilled to be able to say that I currently live an unbusy life, but it was neither easy nor natural for me to reach this point. Ten years ago, my life felt chaotic. At one point during a "Startup Weekend" hackathon, I was at a loss for a way to introduce myself. I worked two part-time jobs (by choice), and I was passionate about both. On top of that, I had a side hustle as a freelance media producer, and as if that weren't enough, I also decided to move from producing media for others to producing for my own online media content subscription business.

So, I'm at a Startup Weekend, and I'm pitching yet another idea for yet another business, and I decided to introduce myself with a bit of snark by saying, "Hello, I'm Andy. I wake up every morning, and I do *stuff*." It worked. People laughed and found it charming and even remembered it months later. It was as if doing stuff (any stuff) was the mark of success somehow. It was as if the sheer volume of my activity demanded a certain amount of respect from a culture obsessed with "the hustle." However, the truth was that my life was a disaster zone of half-baked projects, chronic near misses with deadlines, and unexecuted good ideas. Most days, I felt like I was drowning under the weight of it all.

Add my own chaotic life to the chaos of two young kids and their unpredictable schedules and the demands of renovating a hundred-year-old house always trying to fall apart on me, and the result was that I felt busy all the time. Every night I went to bed with a sigh. I'd lay awake and think to myself; maybe tomorrow I'll make a little progress toward the dreams that matter most. Maybe tomorrow I'll sit down and figure out if I'm devoting enough time to being a good husband and father. Maybe tomorrow I won't feel like I'm falling just a little bit farther behind.

Of course, things don't change just because we wish they would, so I'd wake up every morning without a cohesive structure or design for how to spend my time and channel my energies and mostly react to the demands and priorities of others. I'd spend most of my time trying to make others happy and put out fires that my "freedom" from a schedule inevitably created. Occasionally I'd grow frustrated with the state of things and decide to fire up Netflix and hide from it all for a bit, only to feel worse about myself for my tiny bit of meaningless self-indulgence. You know what I'm talking about. Wash, rinse, repeat, day after day after day.

Then came a moment that triggered a massive change in the way I designed my life. I had been reaching out to others, including a long-time mentor about the fact that my life felt unsustainable. I received some extremely challenging advice about what true freedom means in life. My perspective on time, freedom, and structure was beginning to change, and only a small spark was needed to set my fragile existence aflame clearing the way for a dramatic and sweeping change in the way I lived my life.

That spark came when my wife asked if we could try using breakfast as a way of connecting as a family, even just a couple of times a week. I hate to admit it, but at that moment, I wanted to cry. It seemed like such a simple request, and everything in me wanted to say yes, of course, we can have breakfast together a couple of days every week. And yet I felt so little control over my schedule, and it all felt so unpredictable. I feared that I could never keep it up week after week, and it would end up being just one more way I was failing the people who mattered the most to me. That I could not easily say yes to breakfast together on a couple of scheduled mornings every week felt utterly ridiculous but also seemed to be the ugly truth of the matter. At that moment, this just made me mad. Like *really* mad.

In a fit of rage at the state of my life, I suggested an alternative that may seem counterintuitive but also seemed like our only hope. Instead of scheduling a couple of mornings a week, I suggested that we try doing it every single day. We all ate breakfast every day, why couldn't we commit to eating it together and adding a simple moment of intentional connection? We had grown used to having different morning routines and rhythms because it felt more manageable. Did it have to be that way? We decided to find out. We decided to get up and eat breakfast as early as necessary so that we could do it together every day. I started saying no to meetings over breakfast. We made our intentional connection dead simple and easy to pull off with no forethought. It worked, and eating breakfast together as a family and intentionally connecting before we start our day is still a predictable pattern in our family life several years later.

Eating breakfast together every day may seem like a relatively small thing, but it sparked a revolution in the way I approach my time and the *flow* of time in my life. I asked myself all kinds of questions. Like, why it was easier to do something every morning rather than a couple of unpredictable times a week? I realized that making something a predictable part of my schedule felt great, did this mean I liked structure after all? Should I start scheduling everything? Then again, maybe I should be careful about what gets to be a predictable part of my schedule?

What I learned over time was that it is not enough to have a well-organized schedule or framework for our lives. We can't say yes to everything, so the things that do make it onto the calendar need to matter and help you reliably fill your life with meaning and purpose.

To be clear, this is not a book merely about time-management and how to get things done. These days I am much more concerned about doing the *right* things than doing *more* things. I used to be obsessed with life-hacks and various methods of getting things done. You name it, and I tried it, yet very little stuck in the end. Doing more things was just a way of being lazy about the much harder work of deciding what things were the most important things to spend time on.

This book is about the hard work of declaring the things that matter most to you in life and then designing the flow of your time to ensure you have the freedom to spend as much time as it takes to achieve those important things.

Together we'll discover what matters most to you. You'll unearth and declare a guiding purpose for your life and surround that purpose with values and priorities that ensure you have the capacity you need, to accomplish the big dreams you're currently pushing to the back burner.

I spent vast amounts of time with many different resources to be able to declare a purpose for my life. Then I was still left on my own with the task of designing a life where my time and energy reliably flowed through that purpose. I turned to my interest in the science of physics for help and what I discovered has utterly changed my life and is the primary source of content for this book. I believe it has the potential to change your life too.

To me, it seems obvious to think of time as a flow system. Time flows. Time flows in one direction, moment by moment and day by day. Time flows from the past through the present and into the future. Like a river that gathers capacity through streams and tributaries, we build capacity with the patterns we repeat over and over, day after day. Is your life designed to collect enough capacity in the right areas to accomplish your dreams and goals? Like a river that flows into a lush delta or an estuary full of life, we spend our capacity on productive work. Does what you produce reflect *your* priorities or someone else's?

Flow systems in the natural world like rivers and trees and even the flow systems of our own body are governed by a law of physics that helps them maximize the flow of currents and thrive over time. What if we studied how a river is designed to increase access to its currents? What if we discovered how a tree grows and expands flow capacity year after year for hundreds or even thousands of years? What if we designed a flow system for our lives based on what we learn from nature that will ensure our time flows to what matters now *and* helps us grow our capacity to go after the dreams that seem just out of our reach?

I decided to give it a try. I treated my purpose like the main river through which I would attempt to channel all of my time. This purpose needed to be robust enough to guide my entire life and truly reflect who I am and what I'm wired up to contribute to the world. It couldn't be aspirational, or something that I wish were true of me. It needed to answer the defining question of why I exist and do the things I do. Over time I have developed a way of getting at the answer to this question, and I'm excited to share it with you.

Armed with a sense of purpose, I set out to design a complete flow system for all of my time that gave balance to how I built capacity and how I spent it productively. I trusted the laws of physics that explain the predictable designs of flow systems in nature to give structure to the design of my life. I have dedicated much of the first half of this book to help you make the same discoveries that I have made. I believe it's essential that you have an understanding of why you should design your life in this same way.

It wasn't easy to give structure to my life in this way and then live it out each day. Even though I designed flexibility into the framework with great care, it was still hard to stick to the predictable patterns of a purposefully repetitive structure. I believe this is how we grow and change. It's like building and strengthening an underutilized muscle. Repetition is critical to defining who we are and what we are about in this life. Annie Dillard said it well:

How we spend our days is, of course, how we spend our lives. What we do with this hour, and that one, is what we are doing.

Right. Obvious, no? Of course, what we are doing is what we are doing. Yet who *actually* decides what we are doing? I mean we all make our choices about what to do but who is dictating the priorities that seem to make some options inevitable while others get pushed to the back burner? Is it you *all* of the time. Is it you even *most* of the time? I felt utterly out of control and at the mercy of external priorities nearly all of the time. Because of this, I felt busy and unfulfilled almost all of the time.

On top of all that, our world is full of networked apps and services fighting tooth and nail to capture a share of our available time and attention. We are being pulled into smaller and smaller feedback loops that are hostile to creativity, and work to subvert our natural impulse control. If I had a free moment or two between things I did to please others, I'd fire up twitter or Instagram on my phone or switch over to the ever-present facebook tab in my browser. These networks have no edges. They feel endless, yet they dare us to find the edge that never comes. I was spending much of my "free time" on these platforms and left with nothing meaningful to show for it. I know I'm not alone in this.

So no, it wasn't easy to exert control over the design and structure of my time and follow through with actually living it out. I wish I could say that it was. I wish I could tell you that changing your life in an instant was possible with three easy steps and one weird trick! It's not, and deep down I think we all know that truth. Like anything you want to learn or do, it takes practice. It takes repetition. It takes carefully designed predictable patterns that can guide the flow of your life in spite of the resistance and obstacles that will come your way. Most of all, it takes time. Some things even take large chunks of undistracted time. These rarely come along by chance.

I had big dreams. I dreamed of location-independent income streams so my family could travel and learn from the world before my kids left the house. I dreamed of writing a book. I dreamed of giving large portions of my time to my kids and fostering their dreams as they grow. I dreamed of long hikes in wild places. I dreamed of learning another language. Not one of these dreams made it on to my calendar with regularity, and most had never made it at all. It was as if I was passively waiting for some magic to happen so that I'd suddenly have both the time and the discipline to quit spending time on social media or binge-watching Netflix.

It took hard work to design the flow of my time to make real progress toward these dreams. By making that progress a predictable part of my life, I was surprised by what I could accomplish in a year. We tend to overestimate what we can achieve in a week but vastly underestimate what we can tackle in a year of regular and predictable effort toward our goals and priorities. To sustain that focused effort over long periods takes clarity of purpose and a well-designed flow system for your time. This book will help you get there.

For me, I often work best and am most productive creatively when I have large chunks of unstructured time. It takes a while for my motor to get up to speed and start churning out my best work. Guess what? The only way for me to have these large chunks of unstructured time is to give the rest of my time, the structure necessary to protect the unstructured time! Plus, it's nearly impossible for me to use a large chunk of unstructured time for creativity if I *feel* busy. I need to know the rest of my life is under control and is designed so that time flows to the things that are important to me.

This is what I mean by *unbusy*. It's not about a lack of activity or simply cutting your schedule indiscriminately. Busy is not the same as full. My life is full, and yours should be too. However, it should be full of what is meaningful to you. It should be full of purpose, on purpose. Busy is chaos and reduced capacity. Unbusy is intentional, balanced, and sustainable. Unbusy leads to growth and increased capacity over time. Unbusy is working smarter instead of harder to accomplish more of what you are uniquely designed to contribute with your time and energy.

I accomplish more of what matters most to me now than I ever did when I was working 80+ hours a week at two jobs and a side hustle and feeling insanely busy day after day. Even though I achieve more, I don't feel busy now, and I have a balance between productivity and regeneration. I end each day without regrets about how I spent my time, even if I didn't accomplish everything I wanted to. It's okay because I have a plan to keep allocating the time necessary to build my capacity and to keep going after the priorities that are important to me. The obstacles and diversions of any one given day don't matter in the bigger scheme of things. My time will easily flow around them, and I'll reach my goals anyway.

This is my invitation to you. I invite you on this journey

that leads to an unbusy life. I invite you to have a look at the fascinating physics behind the flow of a river system. Let's learn from the way a tree is designed by nature to move water and nutrients through roots, trunk, branches, and leaves. Let's take a hard look at the obstacles and diversions that are blocking the flow of your time to what matters most and let's make a plan to restore that flow.

We'll start by asking the question of what is. What is your reality? What is your dream? What is your schedule like? How does your time flow (or not flow)? We'll take a look at what it means to feel busy and the gravitational forces that surround us and divert our time away from things that truly matter. We will also have a look at the physics of flow and the reasons behind the easy slide toward chaos and disorder.

From there we'll ask the question of what could be. What could be the shape and design of your life? We'll look around for examples of well-designed flow systems that thrive all around us in the natural world to help us imagine what could be. We'll even look at the physics that explains *why* these natural flow systems thrive over time. We'll spend a lot of time translating what we learn into a tangible design. We'll discover the central guiding purpose through which your time and energy can flow. We'll define values to help you channel your time and to reliably build capacity in the areas that support your purpose in life. Then we'll identify the priorities that give shape to what you produce and create as an expression of your guiding purpose.

Finally, we'll take this design of what your life could be, and we'll make it real by declaring what will be! You will take what you have designed and carefully schedule it into your daily life with reinforcing habits that we'll call *predictable patterns*. These patterns will be attached to your values and priorities so that time flows predictably into and out of these main tributaries of your guiding purpose. Part of declaring *what will be* is the recognition that resistance and obstacles will come our way, and so we'll take time to ensure that we build a *flexible framework* and not a brittle structure that won't hold up to the realities of everyday life. No matter the size of obstacles tossed in your path, your time will be able to flow like a river finding its way around a boulder.

To be unbusy is to be free. Free to design the flow of your life and accomplish your dreams without burning up all of your capacity. It is a radical shift from the status quo of our modern lives. I have taken this radical journey and here's something I've discovered along the way: it's often easier to make sweeping changes than slow and incremental ones. Not *easy*, but easier. It's hard, but hard things inspire us to action! It's going to take a lot of ongoing effort and probably some ongoing support. I'll cover that in the end too. What you need to know is that it's possible. I've done it. I've helped others do it.

This is the journey I'm inviting you on. Will you embark on this journey with me toward an unbusy life where you accomplish more of what truly matters yet feel less busy than you ever thought possible? It's a journey that starts with a rather personal question:

Where do you *really* want to go?

Do The Work:

It takes work to design and live out an unbusy life, so at the end of each chapter, I'll highlight the assignments you need to tackle or ask a reflection question. My goal is to help make the process easier. So if you don't want to stop in the middle of a chapter to "do the work," rest assured that I'll highlight it at the end of each chapter.

For now, though, your only work is to turn the page and keep reading.

2
ENTER YOUR DESTINATION, PLEASE

Where do you want to go?

If you fire up whatever device and app you use to navigate from one place to another—you'll need to answer this question. Where do you want to go? Enter your desired destination, please.

Once you enter a destination, the next steps are reasonably complex, even if today's technology makes it look simple and easy. Assuming that you're starting from your actual physical location on the planet, your device will connect to a network of about 30 satellites orbiting the earth at an altitude of 20,000 km. Once your device has a connection to at least three of these satellites and knows the precise distance you are from each of them based on how long the signal took to reach you, your device can then pinpoint your location using a process known as *trilateration*.

It seems simple enough, right? Except, we're not done.

Because the satellites are experiencing lower gravity in space and moving relative to a clock experiencing gravity on earth, they are subject to the effects of both General Relativity and Special Relativity. In other words, they experience time differently than the atomic clock on earth. Thus the whole GPS network has to make allowances for these effects to figure out accurately where on earth you are.

That leaves the simple matter of analyzing real-time traffic conditions, connecting to route databases, and then plotting the best way for you to get from your location to where you want to go.

Do you know what makes this all work and seem simple in our everyday use of GPS and navigation devices?

Physics.

I am fascinated by physics and have been for as long as I can remember (long before my official introduction to the topic in high school). However, I am not a physicist. Let me get that out of the way up front.

I am a business and leadership coach. I help people get from where they are in life to where they want to be, and I think the laws and language of physics can be surprisingly helpful in getting us there. We depend on physics almost daily to help us navigate our geolocation, why not find out if the concepts of physics can help us navigate other journeys we want to undertake?

Why Physics Though?

You may be fascinated with physics like me or maybe even studied the science extensively, but the odds are stacked against that. Most of you probably go about your daily lives without thinking about physics much and wouldn't be able to name a *Kinematic Equation* to win a game of nerdy trivia. So why use physics to write a book about designing an unbusy life full of meaning and purpose? Because it works.

The tools and concepts in this book consistently help people live more meaningful lives. They have worked for me, and they have worked for my family. We are living the life we've dreamed about for years. We are achieving more of what is truly important to us, and yet we *feel* less busy. I'll tell you more of our story as we journey together in this book, but it's not just us. Through coaching, consulting, and teaching, I have watched these tools and concepts help people all over the world achieve goals, build closer relationships, and find a sense of freedom in their lives.

Our stories are real, and the results are powerful, but you need not only take my word for it. I believe the laws of physics explain how these tools and concepts worked for me and why they'll work for you too.

Physics is one of the most fundamental scientific disciplines. Its main goal is to understand and explain how the universe (and everything in it) behaves. As a part of the universe, physics has a lot to say about us. About how we behave and about how natural forces surround us behave. About how those forces impact our lives and the environments in which we exist.

For instance:

- *Why does the smell of fresh-baked cookies spread throughout the house?* **Physics**.
- *Why does it cost more to cool your home down than it does to heat it?* **Physics**.
- *Why does a blanket warm you up?* **Physics**.

- *And why does sweating cool you down?* **Physics.**
- *How do yoyos work?* **Physics.**
- *How does the battery in your cellphone work? Well... chemistry, but also* **physics!**
- *The shape of a tree?* **Physics.**
- *Why are so many other things shaped like a tree?* **Physics again.**

Have you ever noticed how easy it is to end up with a complicated and disorganized life? Or why pursuing simplicity and order is a whole lot more work? The answer lies in a simple law of physics.

We'll explore this in-depth together. We'll explore how the force of entropy is at work in our world and why it matters that the Second Law of Thermodynamics states that it's always increasing over time. We'll explore a recent and little known addition to the laws of physics, which helps explain how the natural world uses predictable patterns of flow to channel energy and resources in spite of the forces pulling everything toward disorder and chaos.

Fear not, because, even though I'm fascinated by the subject of physics and have done a *lot* of homework to write this book, I still don't understand much of the mathematics behind it all and couldn't even attempt to explain it to you. I will be pursuing simplicity to the edge of offensiveness to a great many theoretical physicists out there. We will use the laws of physics to inform how we design our everyday lives, and we'll trust in the collective work of generations of scientists who do know how and why it all makes sense.

Let me state it plainly; previous knowledge of physics is

not a prerequisite of this book. If you're even just a little bit curious about how a scientific discipline dedicated to explaining the movement, connection and behavior of all things can help us design better lives, then that will be enough to be getting on with.

So with that out of the way, let me return to my original question.

Where do you want to go?

To help you design a lifestyle that will move you from where you are now to the life you've always wanted, we need to know what that life looks like. Later on, I'll introduce some tools that will guide you toward clarity and focus on this subject. For now, though, let's use your imagination.

Imagine tonight when you go to sleep, a miracle happens, and you wake up tomorrow morning to the unbusy life you've always wanted. Only you don't automatically know about the miracle. As you begin your day, how would you know something is different?

Spend some time imagining that day. It's okay to ponder the things you might *have* but pay more attention to *what you do* during that day. Who do you spend it with? Do you go to work every day or is there some other form of income generation? Where on the planet are you? Is this a typical day? How do the next few days look? What about the next few weeks? How do you spend your time? What do you do for fun? How much rest do you get?

It might be just as helpful to ask yourself what you're not spending time on during these days of the life of your dreams.

I encourage you to give this some time and perhaps write

it all down. Don't spend any time worrying about how possible this all is. It was a miracle! Just have fun using your imagination, and we'll worry about reality later. Go wild.

Later on, we'll spend time thinking about the "why" of the things you've imagined. It's incredibly important to know why you do what you do. Will this life you've imagined lead to success in the things that truly matter, or will it end in boredom? It will be essential to our task of designing a meaningful unbusy life that you know your purpose. How else will we create patterns that predictably channel time and energy to achieving that purpose? It's okay if it's all a little fuzzy right now, though. We'll get there.

Keep this dream life handy. We can always correct course or reroute if we need to, but to start this journey, we need to have a general idea of where we're heading. There's one more question we need to answer before we begin in earnest though.

Where are you now?

Do The Work:

Imagine tonight when you go to sleep, a miracle happens, and you wake up tomorrow morning to the unbusy life you've always wanted. Only you don't automatically know about the miracle. As you begin your day, how would you know something is different?

- **Start with the moment you wake up and consider all the details of a morning routine. Take your time and think like a detective. Try to**

discover clues that lead to a discovery of what happened in the night.
- Spend time imagining the details of that day and take notes about what is different.
- You may want to journal a whole day in your unbusy life full of purpose and meaning.

3
LET'S GET REAL

Have you ever tried to pick out a bottle of wine at the supermarket? It can be overwhelming to stand in front of what feels like a never-ending wall of bottles and pretend that you somehow know the difference between them all. Some of you may be aficionados and, armed with the latest ratings from Wine Spectator; you have no trouble weighing the choices to find that perfect bottle to bring to a dinner gathering. The rest of us have little to go on except the pretty labels and the extreme range of prices. Oh look, there are twenty different Cabernet Sauvignons here. The ninety-dollar one must be better than the five-dollar one, right? But is it nearly twenty times better? Heck if I know.

I have friends who routinely spend a hundred dollars or more for a bottle of wine while I'm pretty sure I've never paid over ten. For a long time, I figured my friends were showing off to the point of snobbery. After all, I very much enjoy sipping a glass of my eight dollar California Red at the end of a day and couldn't imagine enjoying a glass very much if I knew it cost me a Benjamin. The truth, it turns out, is much more interesting than mere swagger.

You may have seen the headlines over the years, proving that price alone affects how a wine tastes to us. The first study I came across was published in 2008 by scientists from Cal Tech and Stanford. They had 20 volunteers taste five different wine samples which were identified only by retail prices, ranging from $5 to $90 per bottle. While the subjects were tasting and evaluating the samples, the scientists were busy using fMRI to scan their brain activity.

What I found most interesting is that the subjects consistently reported enjoying the sample from the $90 bottle significantly more than the one from the $10 bottle. As it turns out, both samples came from the same bottle. Hah, I thought, all those wine snobs are mere dupes tricked into enjoying expensive wines by the hit to their pocketbooks! Then I read further into the results of the study.

Plenty of blind taste tests suggested a link between price and enjoyment previously, but this study attempted to measure what was happening in the brains of the subjects. The results are fascinating. When the participants tasted the higher-priced samples, the brain scans recorded increased activity in the area of the brain thought to encode for the pleasantness of an experience.

In other words, the subjects were not just fooling themselves and *saying* they enjoyed the more expensive wines to appear more sophisticated. The perceived price of the wine changes the way our brains encode the positive experience of tasting it.

Almost a decade later, a group of scientists in Europe conducted a similar study armed with better technology and significant advances in our understanding of how the human brain works. The study included 30 subjects, and they tasted three samples labeled with bottle prices from 3 to 18 euros. All three samples were from the same bottle, and yet the brain scans showed definitively that our brains manipulate the experience of tasting wine based on the perceived price.

Perception *is* reality.

I have regularly said this a bit tongue-in-cheek over the years. *Perception is reality — wink, wink.* As if enlightened minds (like mine) could easily overcome this tendency of our brains to equate what it merely perceives with actual reality. Please forgive my rather blatant and disgusting arrogance. While I do believe we can work to change our perceptions and gain new frames of reference, it is far from simple. For the most part, there is no difference between what we perceive moment by moment and objective reality. It's simply how our brains work *chemically* and just knowing what's going on doesn't change things a whole lot.

So What's My Point?

I bring all this up because we're about to take a long hard look at your time and how you currently spend it. I want you to remember that how you *feel* about your time *is* your reality. Not just at some superficial level either. I'm not trying to humor you with a sense of validation. I'm merely stating the scientific truth that how we feel about or perceive our time has the power to affect our brain chemistry with genuine and often physical consequences. How you feel about your time, whether busy and hurried or relaxed and balanced, is your reality.

A majority of Americans report *feeling* like they don't have enough time to get everything done each day. It doesn't matter that the actual statistics say we have more free time than ever. We feel busy, and that leads to stress, anxiety, and cascading effects on our health and well-being. It also tends to have dramatic effects on our relationships with each other. It may sound weirdly subjective for a book focused on using physics to design an unbusy life to suggest, but it's more important at this point, to be honest about how we *feel* rather than analyze the nitty-gritty of our schedules to look for wasted time. If you feel "crunched for time," then you are. It's as simple as that.

So what does it mean to be crunched for time? John Robinson, researcher, and author of *Time For Life* has been studying how people spend time for decades. Long ago, he noticed the disconnect between how people objectively spent their time and how they felt about it. He came up with a ten-question "Time Crunch Scale" to help evaluate the otherwise subjective area of how people feel about their available time. I think it's helpful and I'd like you to take some time to process this slightly altered version as honestly as you can. Make a note of whether you agree or disagree with each of the following statements:

1. I often feel under stress when I don't have enough time.
2. When I need more time, I tend to cut back on my sleep.
3. At the end of the day, I often feel that I haven't accomplished what I set out to do.
4. I worry that I don't spend enough time with my family or friends.
5. I feel that I'm constantly under stress — trying to accomplish more than I can handle.
6. I feel trapped in a daily routine.
7. When I'm working long hours, I often feel guilty that I'm not at home.
8. Sometimes I feel that my spouse doesn't know who I am anymore.
9. I often feel rushed, even to do the things I have to do.
10. I just don't have time for fun anymore.

If reported statistics hold, then many of us agreed with nearly all of these statements. Many more agree with at least a few and almost nine in ten of us would report "often feeling rushed, even to do the things I have to do." Most of us feel some level of *time famine*. We do not think we have enough time for all the things we feel the need to do. We feel like we are *starving* for time. These feelings have serious consequences.

For instance, let's look at number ten. If you don't think

you have enough time for fun anymore, then it's likely you are quite actually unable to enjoy the time that is meant to be fun with your family or friends. All of this will likely lead to worry and stress about spending enough time with them since you *perceive* the time you do spend as inferior in quality. This feeling of anxiety may lead to a conscious decision to cut back on sleep or even just a reduction in sleep quality because at the end of the day you're pretty sure you haven't accomplished what you set out to do. Rush. Strive. Worry. More Stress. The cycle continues and amplifies, and you feel trapped in a daily routine that isn't accomplishing what you want out of life.

Not to mention the fact that it is a challenge to use time well if we are constantly worrying about how we'll have time to get everything else that matters done. It's nearly impossible to spend time for rest and restoration of our capacity and energy when we feel like it comes at the expense of getting something else important done. Feeling guilty about time spent on rest leads to lives that are massively out of balance, which leads to burnout and reduced capacity. It doesn't matter whether you objectively have time for rest or not. If you don't *feel* like you have time, you won't be able to spend time on the things that build your capacity. If you don't use time well for restoration, then, in the long run, you will end up with reduced capacity and accomplish less no matter how hard you work.

As I said before and I'm sure you have noticed, all of these statements are a bit subjective and based on how we feel about time. This subjectivity is helpful because we tend to be pretty bad at guessing accurately about how we actually spend our time and how much we have available. However, it doesn't matter very much how bad we are at mentally keeping track of our time because if our perception is that we're always rushing around and busy to the point of increasing worry and stress, well then, that's our reality right?

How we feel about our time *is* our reality.

What Does The Data Say?

Conventional wisdom says we are busy and over-scheduled people, everyone knows that. Alexis de Tocqueville observed more than 150 years ago that "The American is always in a hurry." Certainly, things have only gotten worse with all of our technology and notifications vying for our attention. With the increase in two-income households and the amount of extra-curricular activities these days, we must be more pressed for time. What about the intense competition of the global economy? Certainly, we must all be working longer hours to keep up? There must be stacks and stacks of books about how out of balance our lives are, never mind the magazine and newspaper articles. They can't all be wrong, can they?

If how we feel about our time is our reality, then they aren't wrong. However, according to decades of research and multiple studies, there exist significant discrepancies between how we feel about our time and the data recording how we actually spend it. The truth may be surprising. You probably aren't as busy as you think you are. On average, we have more free time today than in previous generations.

When it comes to spending time with our kids, the trend is also positive even though we *feel* like we're dropping the ball on that front, which leads to worry. When it comes to time and quality of life, we are trending upwards on all fronts versus a generation or two ago. So why doesn't it feel that way?

A big reason has to do with how we experience time in our minds. The way time passes in our minds is subjective and has a lot to do with how we feel about the activity we're engaged in. An hour spent waiting in line at the DMV feels a lot longer than an hour spent doing something we enjoy. The science is in; time does indeed fly when we're having fun! This perception difference leads to resentment and intensely negative feelings about time we feel has been wasted and thus overshadows a similar chunk of time we may consider well-spent. At the end of the day, negative emotions or feelings of failure will loom larger in our minds than even the same amount of time spent accomplishing a goal or engaged in something we value. All of this is especially true if we feel a lack of control over the structure of our days, a problem we will address in later chapters.

On top of that, we all face an ever-increasing amount of social pressure fed by our 'social' feeds. Our time fractured and atomized by our hectic pace of life. As a result, we turn more and more to the social media apps on our devices to pass the small gaps in our schedules that count as "free time." We tell ourselves that it's the only way of keeping up relationships with friends and family since we have no time to spend with them face to face. These apps present us with a never-ending stream of people who seem to be better at spending their time than us. People who appear to have time to exercise. People who have time to adventure with their families. People who are succeeding more than us at work. People who *appear* to have perfect kids. People who have time to *do* all the fantastic Pinterest projects instead of just filling up their boards with aspirations.

How we feel about our time is our reality. While we're stealing a few moments mashing the like button and scrolling through the endless feeds presented to us by our new algorithmic overlords, we're left feeling like we don't measure up. It's no wonder most of us end our day feeling like we didn't have the time to accomplish everything we set out to do. There is simply no way around it; you and I will never measure up to the curated and addictive feeds presented by the algorithms. However, we can define what truly matters to us and design a life that channels our time and energy toward those things in a predictable way. In the end, as we'll learn from the predictable patterns of design in nature, the key to designing the life you want is all about finding a healthy balance. And the need for moderation is especially real for time spent on social media.

There's one more factor driving our tendency toward feeling crunched for time, and it's perhaps the most insidious. Being busy has become a key symbol or marker of status and success in our culture. Since the Industrial Revolution, our relationship with time has been rapidly evolving. Somewhere along the line, time *became* money, and our relationship with rest and recreation also shifted. For centuries a key marker of wealth and success was time for leisure. Accumulated wealth enabled time for restorative activities that had nothing to do with income generation.

These days time is sacrificed on the altar of productivity.

It is those who have the most money rather than available time whom we consider successful. Thus the wealthiest people among us appear to be the busiest. They pack their schedules and forgo vacation in an attempt to extract maximum *financial* value from every last second. Being busy is now synonymous with success. Someone asks us, "how's it going?" The answer is "busy." This answer has become so ubiquitous that we often skip the back and forth and ask each other, "are you staying busy?" We fill our minutes and seconds with 'productive' activity, so the answer is always, "yes." It would be embarrassing to say that in fact, we are not busy. It would be like admitting that we are failing somehow.

In our world, an unbusy life feels abnormal or even irresponsible. A busy life is a normal life. To escape this cultural norm, we need a new relationship with both time and money. We need to learn to see time as a currency separate from money and place it along a spectrum of value with other currencies like wisdom and relationships. I'll give you the tools to do just that.

There is hope.

It's possible at this point that you're feeling a bit overwhelmed. However, in all of this, I see a great deal of hope. I look at the data and see an opportunity. You probably have more time than you think you do. The prevailing design that imposes itself on our lives is one that values being busy over everything else. We need a new design paradigm, and the truth is that you probably have more control over the design of your schedule than you imagine. There is no question that some of us may need to do less. All of us need to ask if we're doing the *right* things. Every one of us will be able to design a life in which we accomplish more of the things that truly matter and *feel* less busy at the same time. Redesigning the flow of your time will change everything because how you feel about your time is your reality.

I know this because I used the tools and concepts introduced in this book to design a life in which I am accomplishing more of my goals and dreams than I ever thought possible and yet I feel less busy then I did before. For years now, I have been able to honestly say that I disagree with all ten of the questions on the time crunch scale. There are still days when I have to agree with question three, but it's almost always because of poor choices I made on that particular day. Or sometimes, I'm just overly optimistic about what I can get done in a day. However, I've noticed another surprising truth. I tend to underestimate what I can achieve in a few months of consistently living with a flexible framework of predictable patterns that channel my time to the things I value and the goals I've set. Having observed this, I don't worry about any given day when I feel like I didn't have enough time.

I'm not telling you this to brag. For most of my life, I would have strongly agreed with most of those questions. My work life gave me complete control over my schedule, and yet I was always frustrated and worried about a lack of progress toward the significant goals in all areas of my life. Any structure felt like a straight jacket to me. I wanted to be free to use my time how I saw fit on any given day. I avoided advanced planning like the plague. I had massive amounts of unstructured time which I thought gave me freedom. I was free to drop whatever I happened to be doing and grab lunch at a moment's notice. However, in reality, that didn't happen very much. I was free to wake up every morning and decide what was most important to work on that day. However, I often felt paralyzed by the task of deciding what to do every day. Without any sort of pattern or framework to guide my days, I was constantly distracted by outside forces. The truth is, I had plenty of time, but it didn't *feel* like I did. I always worried if I was doing the right things with my time.

I often felt like a failure. I thought that I had complete freedom. I thought, perhaps I'm just not cut out to handle life without someone else telling me what to do all the time. Why am I continually staying up late to meet deadlines? Why can't I get it together and finish projects on time? I'm the only one telling me what to do, so why am I always worried if I'm doing the right things? In dark personal moments, I seriously considered giving up the 'freedom' I had to go work in a factory. At least I could leave at the end of the workday and not worry if there was more work to be done that day.

I was too proud to admit most of this out loud to others. I often fiercely defended my lifestyle and protected the unstructured nature of my schedule. *Don't tell me what to do!* I would scream in my head when well-meaning people would attempt to impose order on my chaotic life. Then one day, all my defenses came tumbling down over a simple conversation with a trusted mentor. We were chatting about why I resisted structure and what it truly means to be free. He made a simple proclamation that pierced my soul and completely changed my life. He said,

The opposite of structure is *not* freedom; it's chaos.

He let that sink in for a while. Then in a moment of mental jujitsu, he used my love for physics against me, "It's a basic law of the universe that all things tend from structure and order toward chaos, right?" Damn, I thought. He's right.

Do The Work:

It's essential to know how you *feel* about your time, so if you haven't taken the time to consider your answers to the Time Crunch Scale, do it now:

1. I often feel under stress when I don't have enough time.
2. When I need more time, I tend to cut back on my sleep.
3. At the end of the day, I often feel that I haven't accomplished what I set out to do.
4. I worry that I don't spend enough time with my family or friends.
5. I feel that I'm constantly under stress — trying to accomplish more than I can handle.
6. I feel trapped in a daily routine.
7. When I'm working long hours, I often feel guilty that I'm not at home.
8. Sometimes I feel that my spouse doesn't know who I am anymore.

9. I often feel rushed, even to do the things I have to do.
10. I just don't have time for fun anymore.

Reflection Question:

How would you describe freedom from the perspective of time and your schedule?

4
ENTROPY AND THE 2ND LAW

I grew up along the sandy shores of Lake Michigan. When the waves were up, my family and I spent countless hours at the beach body surfing. If the lake were calm, we would build ever more elaborate sandcastles when they weren't. We were serious about our sand structures. Plastic beach shovels were for amateurs, so we brought along our sturdy landscaping tools, masonry trowels, and spray-bottles to aid in our sculpting.

We were a real-life Brady Bunch, and occasionally all six siblings were united by a single vision. We would spend dozens of "work-hours" in a single day to dig a lagoon and build up exotic structures to line our new waterfront properties. Eventually, though the food we also dragged along with us across the hot sand would run out and we'd be forced to leave to find more sustenance.

Sometimes we'd get to come right back the next morning for another day at the beach. Though we would always look, inevitably we'd find only the barest evidence of our efforts from the previous day. Not one of us was surprised by this fact. Our creations would succumb to the wind and the waves, reduced to unrecognizable lumps in the sand, and this seemed self-evident and ordinary. So banal that no comment or conversation was needed on the subject. Sandcastles disappeared by the next morning; this was just the way the world worked. We built a structure on the beach one day, and it was reduced to lumpy sand by the next.

Do you know what would have surprised the heck out of us? We would have been stunned to arrive after a particularly stormy night to find that the forces of nature had assembled an intricate sandcastle all on their own. Even as kids, we knew that the odds of that happening were so high that we'd consider it impossible. Even casual observers of the world around us know that well-ordered gardens give way to weeds and chaos. Or that without maintenance, buildings will eventually crumble and decay. Mountains erode, their sharp edges being ground by time into gentle hills. A bucket full of ice and water will end up just a bunch of lukewarm water. Without extra effort, things tend to fall apart.

This is how things work, but have you ever asked why? It's okay if you haven't, but I wanted to illustrate the fact that you do already know much of the physics we'll be talking about in this book. You may even consider it "common sense," and to a certain extent, that's undoubtedly true. But if we dig a little deeper into these principles of physics, we will recognize the way they influence everything around us—even our own lives. These discoveries will have a profound impact. So I hope you'll stick with me as I dive into the details of why a sandcastle disappears overnight and is never spontaneously formed without effort. As I promised, I'll keep it as simple as possible, and there will be no test at the end!

To get started, I have to introduce a few concepts that usually fall within the specific discipline of *thermodynamics*. You've probably heard of thermodynamics but might not know what it means precisely. Very simply stated, it's a branch of physics that studies the relationship between different forms of energy. The reason I want to take a look at it together is that our goal is to channel the energy available to us toward the things that truly matter to us. You may not be paying much attention to the concepts of thermodynamics right now. However, you and I are very much impacted by them every moment of every day. So before we venture forth and start designing solutions to the flow of energy in our lives, we should get acquainted with how the flow of energy works in our universe. I'll keep the introduction simple. I promise it will help in the long run!

What is entropy?

The first concept we need to look at is called *entropy*.

Entropy is a measurement of the disorder of a given system. Now, this might bring to mind visions of "messy" systems such as a messy room, but "disorder" is a more accurate idea. So instead of thinking of a room that looks messy to us, it would be slightly better to think of how *mixed-up* all the different items in that room are. While it can be popular to talk about entropy as a force with ill intent hell-bent on the destruction of everything, that's not really how it works. It's a whole lot less scary than that. It's actually a *measure-*

ment of an overwhelmingly persistent force at work in our universe. Stick with me while I try to demystify it a bit.

A simple way to illustrate entropy is to imagine a box full of puzzle pieces. There exists only one specific state in which all those puzzle pieces will fit together and form the picture on the front of the box. Imagine we took the box full of puzzle pieces, shook it up and dumped it out onto a table. We would be shocked if all the pieces were to *spontaneously* fall into place, creating the finished version of the puzzle. Let's talk about why.

The truth is—and this may cause some disbelief—that all of the puzzle pieces landing in the perfect finished positions is just as likely an outcome as whatever *specific individual configuration* that we get. Don't get all bent out of shape about the pieces snapping together since gravity can't overcome the friction of the fit. I'm merely talking about the order and placement in which they end up. So why doesn't it ever actually happen? Well, the answer is just statistics and probability. There is only one possible configuration that looks ordered to us, while there are a great many possible configurations that look like disorder to us. In fact, with a 2000 piece puzzle, there are more possible configurations that look disordered to us than atoms in the observable universe! The odds against that one ordered configuration are *literally* astronomical. Yet each individual configuration is just as likely as the next.

Actually, I'm getting ahead of myself. Entropy doesn't really tell us why the pieces never end up in the proper place and order because it is merely the *measurement* of possible configurations of an overall result. With our puzzle example, there are just two overall results, the finished puzzle, and chaos. The entropy of the completed puzzle is low because there is a tiny number (only one) of possible configurations to achieve that result. The entropy of a chaotic mess of puzzle pieces is high because there are so many possible configurations that look like a chaotic mess to us. So entropy is just a way to tell how many possibilities exist for different overall results in a random system.

Let's imagine one more scenario that will prove more useful for the next concept that I need to introduce.

Imagine you're standing in the corner of a decent sized room filled with people. Over in the opposite corner, someone just lit a cigarette and is exhaling their first inhalation. At this moment all of the smoke particles are over in that corner of the room, and though you may be able to see them, you can't smell them. At this moment, the entropy of those smoke particles is low. There are a small number of possible configurations of those particles which will allow you to see them in that far corner and not smell them in yours. We know this won't last. The smoke particles have the freedom to bounce around in that room randomly, and the number of possible configurations where they "fill" the space is extremely high. The possibility that they end up all in the far corner is remote, to say the least. The entropy is thus high when all the smoke is mixed up into the entire room.

The 2nd Law

We all instinctively know that the smoke exhaled in one corner of a room will end up filling the room. We also know that it won't end up spontaneously all back into that one corner that it started in. The thing is, it wouldn't be *impossible* for it to happen. That is to say; it wouldn't break any of the physical laws of the universe as we understand them. It *could* happen, so why is it that we never actually see this possibility in real life? Probability and statistics.

The 2nd Law of Thermodynamics states what we already know: a closed system will always move toward the state for which there are many possible "arrangements" that look the same to us. Never the other way around. There are many, many arrangements of the smoke particles throughout a room that ends up looking the same to us (i.e., the room is filled with smoke). The number of arrangements that put all the particles back in the first corner is relatively small. In fact, it's so tiny compared to the smoke filling the room that physicists have decided the odds can be safely ignored.

The 2nd Law is a statement of overwhelming probability. The probability of disorder, chaos, and equilibrium (things being equally mixed-up) are so high that systems will always tend in that direction without outside input.

It is the reason why if we place ice cubes in a glass of water, we know we'll eventually end up with just a glass of water. It's why neat and tidy rooms subject to a morning of playtime end up looking messy and disordered to us. It's why a well-tended garden will end up a weed-filled nightmare after long summer vacations. It's also why a sandcastle built with extreme care will inevitably end up as a patch of lumpy sand the next day.

The 2nd Law also explains why it's so much easier to increase entropy (disorder) than it is to decrease it. For example, it's a whole lot easier to break an egg than it is to "unbreak" it—like *a lot* easier. It's easier to mix cream into coffee and nearly impossible to separate the two. The 2nd Law also explains why it takes less energy to heat things than to cool them down. I'm not going to go into it though; you'll just have to trust me.

Things tend toward disorder and chaos because it requires almost no effort. To go the other way, to bring order and structure to things does require effort. Typically a disproportionate *amount* of effort.

What does this have to do with designing an unbusy life? Quite a lot actually. Take a moment to consider the state of your schedule. How do you feel about your time? Does your life feel chaotic? Does it feel out of your control sometimes? Does it feel like a puzzle with all the pieces fitting nicely to create a picture of your best life? Or, does it feel more like all the pieces have just been dumped unceremoniously in a big mess on the table?

If you feel like your life is a bit chaotic and messy, how much work did it take on your part for it to end up that way? Probably not much. It's just the natural way of things, and it's essential to understand why. There are way more possible scenarios where your life ends up chaotic than the few that result in your time flowing reliably toward the things that matter most to you.

Now ask yourself, what would it take to make your schedule feel simple and well ordered? A lot of effort, right? This difference is what I'm trying to explain with this section on entropy. We are going to do the work. The first step is deciding that a better life is worth the effort of fighting back against the natural force of entropy in our lives. It's hard work, but it is possible.

And yet, there is hope.

Even though the universe is naturally moving toward disorder on a long time-scale, we can expend effort and fight back against the overwhelming odds of increasing entropy. On top of that, the result is often quite satisfying and fulfilling because of the effort involved. Consider our puzzle, for example. Finishing a 2000 piece puzzle is far more challenging than finishing one with only 50 pieces. However, it is that much more rewarding because of the effort required to bring about order and structure from the initial chaos.

In fact, the more unlikely a thing is in the face of the universe's relentless march toward chaos, the more likely we are to consider it beautiful and precious.

This year I was lucky enough to visit Sequoia National Park and spend whole days walking among the truly incredible "big trees" which grow there. I was brought to tears by the knowledge of how unlikely such life is in the universe the vast energy collected and channeled over thousands of years. There are so many other ways the atoms caught up in the structure of those trees could be arranged. They should not exist, and yet my family and I were able to walk among thousands of them. Words seem utterly inadequate to express how beautiful they seemed to me.

Or consider the human body. There are a great many possible configurations of the atoms that make up your particular body. Nearly all of them would result in no life at all, let alone the specific entity that is you. At a cosmological scale, the odds against your existence are incredibly steep, and yet here you are reading this sentence. Given what we have managed to learn and observe about the universe, life is indeed precious. On the one hand, there could be no life without the conditions of the universe and its ever-increasing entropy over time. On the other hand, all life must eventually succumb to the inevitability of that very same pull of entropy increasing.

Entropy giveth and entropy taketh away.

So how is it that in a universe that is accelerating toward the ultimate chaos—the disordered dissipation of all free energy—we have such remarkable examples of beautifully intricate life. Things such as sequoias and humans and even butterflies and bumblebees?

The answer is that we live in a particularly vibrant moment of cosmological history. Despite the universe's overall march toward higher entropy and dissipation, there are still many pockets of free (useful) energy bouncing around. On top of that, the universe has developed predictable patterns of design for channeling that energy in ways that result in complex and wondrous features of the natural world around us, including life itself.

Whenever we look closely at systems that persist over time and which grow and evolve in spite of the 2nd Law, we see a familiar pattern. It is the pattern of life but also of efficient natural and mechanical systems here on earth and beyond. It's at work in your body right now, though it's unlikely you've ever heard of it.

It is a relatively new law of physics with very low name recognition, but it explains a great deal of what we see and experience in our everyday lives.

The basic premise of this book is that this newish law

can help us design our lives in a way that will help us fight back against the pull of chaos and disorder. And not merely resist, we can use it to design and achieve the life of our dreams.

Do The Work:

Reflection Questions:

1. Think about the state of your schedule. How easy would it be for your life to become even more complicated?
2. What steps do you imagine it would take to simplify your life dramatically?

5

THE PREDICTABLE PATTERN OF DESIGN IN NATURE

Have you ever noticed how many things around us are shaped like a tree? Take a moment and look around you. Inside a building, or out in nature, it makes little difference. The branching tree-like structure of the world around us is hard to unsee once you begin to take notice.

Consider how the tree we see above ground is mirrored by the same pattern below. Or the watershed that flows from creek to tributary to river and on to a tree-shaped delta. Or the electricity flowing into your home and the various *branch* circuits. It is the same with the flow of freshwater or the plumbing that carries the wastewater from drain pipes to the sewer pipe. Then there is our own body, both our circulatory system and the airways in our lungs share the same tree-like pattern. A bolt of lighting, computer circuitry, fungal mycelium, traffic patterns, the list goes on and on. The design is evident, but *why*?

People have been asking this question for ages, and until

quite recently the consensus was that it is merely a coincidence. As recently as September of 1995 scientists gathered from around the world for a conference in Nancy, France on thermodynamics. The pre-banquet speech was given by Nobel laureate Ilya Prigogine, in which he echoed the accepted conventional wisdom of the scientific community. Yes, tree-shaped patterns abound in nature, but they are nothing but the result of chance, a "roll of the dice," he said. I don't mean to throw a brilliant man under the bus by highlighting what we now tend to dismiss as folly. I could cite dozens of other men and women who expressed the same sentiment with certainty throughout much of the twentieth century. This story only stands out because of another scientist who was present at that conference, heard that speech, and disagreed.

Also in attendance to give a lecture at this conference was a Romanian born, MIT trained, Duke University professor of mechanical engineering. His name is Adrian Bejan, and just before arriving at the event, he had been working on the increasingly difficult problem of passively cooling computer chips. For years, electronics had been decreasing in size while computational power was increasing, creating an excess of heat in a shrinking amount of space. The time of blowing air across chips to remove heat was ending, and engineers were seeking ways of channeling that heat away from chips with other methods. Adrian Bejan developed a technique of placing channels of thermally conductive materials directly onto the chips. After calculating the most efficient pattern of placement for these channels, he noticed that it resembled the tree-like flow structures so prevalent in nature. These observations and the reasons why his design should mirror the design of flow systems in nature began percolating in the back of his mind.

And so it was that while listening to that speech in Nancy, he experienced a sudden moment of realization. The conventional wisdom was wrong. Something was responsible for the repeated pattern of geometry. These branching configurations of flow in both animate and inanimate systems were not just the result of cosmic coincidence. The problem was that no law, theory, or principle in science could explain it. Yet.

On a newfound mission to explain what seemed like a coincidence to others, Adrian put pen to paper during the plane ride home. He wrote down what he then called the Constructal Theory and would later become known as the Constructal Law:

> For a finite-size flow system to persist in time (to live), its configuration must evolve freely in such a way that it provides greater and greater access to the currents that flow through it.

Because this is written in the dispassionate language of science, it may seem a bit vague and uninspired. I assure you it's an idea with immense value to our world and our lives. Let's break it down a bit and dig in. Everything that moves is a flow system. That means animate things like plants and animals are flow systems (actually most are flow systems made up of many smaller flow systems). It also means that inanimate things (both natural and constructed) like rivers, lava flows, electrical grids, and sewers are flow systems. All of these systems vary primarily because of what and how much flows through them. Defining a "finite-sized" flow system can get a bit tricky. We're going to stick to the very basic idea of something with a flowing current and a design through which it flows. That will be plenty for us to move forward.

For example, a river system has a current of water that flows through it and a design consisting of streams and tributaries at the headwaters, the main river, and the branching design of the delta. You could zoom out and talk about the entire system of water flowing inside the global hydrosphere, but it's hard to pin that down to a single design. A river is a finite-sized flow system and is therefore subject to the Constructal Law, while the global hydrosphere is not finite-sized and is subject to a whole lot more.

The next part of the idea is about how we define life. Constructal Law redefines life as anything that moves, and why not? Movement is already one of the fundamental signs of biological life. If a current continues to move through a flow system, then it lives. If the current ceases, then it dies. A flowing river is alive. A dried-up riverbed is dead, from the perspective of the river as a system that flows. If blood and oxygen flow through an organism, it lives. If they stop flowing, the organism is dead. The rest of the Constructal Law is going to explain to us how a flow system continues to live and thrive and even grow. This is what it means to "persist in time."

Life is flow, and life is also design; which is what the next part of the statement is telling us. The flow system has a "configuration," and that is to say, a design through which something flows. The design will depend on what is flowing, where it is flowing, and what resistance and obstacles are encountered.

This flexibility is what the *freedom to evolve* part of the statement is getting at. The world around us is full of constraints that prevent systems from organizing themselves into more and more efficient ways of flowing. A landslide might block a river's most efficient configuration, or other competing flow systems might impose resistance on any number of systems in their path. So to live and thrive, a system must have the freedom to evolve toward some purpose.

What is that purpose? To "provide greater and greater access to the currents that flow through it." This part means the purpose of any flow system is to maximize the rate of currents that flows through it. All this means that a flow system will develop shape and structure and evolve (if given freedom) to minimize the resistance that will inevitably work against it. For example, a small rivulet of rainwater running down a slope can only carry so much current. Before long it will join with others to form a creek, and if the rain continues to fall, that creek will join with others to create a river. Even the river's shape will change and evolve as more and more tributaries join it to provide easier access to currents of water flowing through it.

Keep this in mind as we begin to move forward and design the flow of our time toward what matters most. It will be essential that we give our designs the freedom to evolve so that resistance and obstacles don't build up and block our well-intentioned plans. We'll return to these ideas in more detail in the next few chapters.

All of this may seem like common sense to you, but it answers the question of why designs like this are so prevalent and not only in nature. Even as humans seek to develop increasingly efficient designs for things that flow, like traffic and heat, we frequently end up with designs that obey this principle. It not only tells us why but also allows us to predict how things *should* be designed. For instance, if we consider the system of flow that should be designed to carry rainwater falling on an area of land to the ocean, we would be solving a problem not so different than the flow of heat away from a computer chip. There are other principles at work here like fluid dynamics and a whole lot of math, and I promised to keep things simple.

So let me just say that when you do the math, you'll find that the best way to maximize the flow from an area (rainwater falling on a hillside) to a point (river mouth into the sea) is to move with many small and slow channels that form branches of fewer and fewer but more substantial and faster channels of flow. It's the same for any "area to point" or "point to area" flow system, which is why a river system, our lungs, our circulatory system, and the CPU cooling design all look like a tree to us. It's a good design for moving current from a large distributed area to a point (river to river mouth) or from a point to a distributed area (our mouth to the alveoli of our lungs).

Of course, a "point to point" flow system would evolve differently, but since our daily lives resemble an "area to point" flow of time and energy, we're going to stick with tree-shaped flow systems.

Some would no doubt like to jump in here and claim that time is more like a linear "point to point" flow system. I can sympathize with this view, but that's an unhelpful way to look at our lives or our schedule of time. There is some physics I could throw at you right now about space and time, but I'm not going to get side-tracked. Plus, I'm saving space-time as a treat for the end of the book.

So let's do this, think about your time as an area like the page of a calendar. There are many ways that time can be collected and channeled from that area toward the things that you value and truly matter to you. In this way, our lives and available time resemble an "area to point" or even an "area to point to area" flow system.

How Come?

So, the Constructal Law causes flow systems to generate better and better flowing designs, which begs the question: What causes the Constructal Law? The truth is, we don't know. That may sound strange, but it's more common in science than you might imagine. Constructal Law, along with things like gravity, the freezing point of water, and Newton's laws of motion are what we call "first principles." That means they cannot be arrived at or derived from other scientific laws. It's just the way our world is, and we don't know why. We know that anything with mass generates a gravitational field. How come? That we don't know. What we do know is how gravity works and why objects fall when pushed off a table. It's useful then to summarize and define these first principles even if we don't know why the universe includes them.

For an idea like this to become accepted as a law of science, it must first accurately and concisely summarize vast amounts of observational evidence surrounding natural phenomena of the same kind. However, it must be set free from the realm of observation. Armed only with this statement of a fundamental truth about the phenomena, we must be able to preemptively predict what the right design is for a given flow system. Once we have determined what that design is with only a pencil and paper (or supercomputer if necessary), we can then go back out into the world to see if our predictions prove to be correct. Predict and then verify. Predict and then verify, over and over again to see if the idea holds up in every case. If it doesn't, then we don't have a new law of physics.

Let's consider a much older law to get a better picture. The law of conservation of energy states that energy can neither be created nor destroyed; instead, it can only be transformed or transferred from one form to another. We tend to take this for granted now, but it took many centuries of observations, empirical evidence, and theories that were circling the eventual idea that we have come to consider a basic law of the physical universe. Eventually, in the 18th and 19th centuries, we gave up the theory that heat was a fluid (see "caloric theory" if you're interested) and recognized it as a predictable form of energy conversion. Armed with new quantifiable and predictable equations of energy conversion and kinetic energy potential (work), engineers began to design more efficient engines through scientific methods rather than tinkering with trial and error. That is the benefit of summarizing overwhelming observations into a fundamental law describing how things work. We can work out better designs on paper based on these laws and equations, and then build them to verify that our understanding of these first principles is accurate.

Even in today's fast-paced world of science in technology, the Constructal Law is still in its infancy. That's not to say that it hasn't been subjected to a great deal of scrutiny and testing by scientists around the world because it certainly has. In the decades since it was first published, it has been used to examine flow systems of every kind. Every time, researchers have been able to use the Constructal Law to predict the design, and verify it with observation. However, things are just getting started with this cutting edge idea. Welcome to the ground floor!

So, the Constructal Law accurately explains the predictable pattern of design that we observe in nature. Beyond that, we can use it to understand why designs emerge where they do, and also we can predict how the design of flow systems will evolve in the future. That is powerful. We begin to see these patterns of design, even in places where we didn't expect. For instance, Dr. Bejan and his colleagues have used Constructal Law to explain how societal organization has evolved, and it's distribution across the globe.

Once we see the Constructal Law at work all around, we can see the result of millions of years of relentless refinements in the flow systems that surround us. We can study how systems generate shape and structure and how they evolve to overcome obstacles and thrive in a universe filled with resistance. We can take what we learn and use it to improve the designs dramatically we create for the flow of useful currents in our world.

For instance, once we understand the ratios of short and slow types of flow, to the fast and long types of flow in something like a river basin, we discover a pattern designed for maximum efficiency. We use those ratios to predict the most efficient flow of traffic from a wide area such as an entire metropolitan area to the dense urban core. If we compare that prediction to the actual flows of traffic that result from the existing transportation design, we are likely to find areas where the flow can be improved. Not only that, but we can predict how the transportation system will need to evolve, in connection with the expected growth of communities around the entire area.

This works for traffic flows of all kinds from theme parks to airport terminals and from global air traffic to supply chains. Anything that moves and flows obeys the Constructal Law, yet we often are responsible for the resistance that prevents better designs. We design an airport without much thought to passenger flow from arrival to departure gates. The design is not free to evolve as needed because it would be too costly, so like a dammed-up river, the current gets blocked. On the other hand, the street grid that we often take for granted as a feature of modern cities is a superb design for letting traffic patterns evolve in time as needed by the people and vehicles of the city. Consider the shape of traffic descending upon a sporting stadium from all over the city, what would it look like? It would look like a tree or a river basin with many small and slow streams of traffic coming from side streets joining faster and longer roads all feeding to a single point.

Researchers also use Constructal Law to study and predict the flow of information and ideas. What are the pathways and channels for the flow of something less tangible like discoveries or political ideology? Or what about the evolution of culture and societal organization?

Researchers have mapped the flow of human civilization and compared the accumulation of cities large and small to the distribution of trees of various sizes in a forest.

I share these examples to show that flows of current are everywhere but aren't always as obvious as the river flowing on its way to the sea.

One of those less apparent currents is the flow of time. Specifically, I'm interested in exploring the flow of time and energy in my life and yours. I mentioned in chapter three that most of us reach the end of each day feeling like we didn't have enough time to accomplish what we wanted to. Our daily, weekly, and annual schedules make up the channels through which our time and energy flow, yet most of us feel a lack of control over our routines. Like a river blocked and diverted, the landscape of our lives is full of friction, resistance, and blockages.

Day by day and year by year, our time is a flow system which we either design freely or else it's designed for us by circumstances that may seem out of our control. You have more freedom than you may imagine. Obstacles have likely forced complex and inefficient patterns of flow in your life. Let's give ourselves the freedom to evolve and design rhythms and routines that provide greater access to the flow of time and energy to the things that truly matter to us.

It's time to consider the pattern of your life as it is and then use the predictable pattern of design that surrounds us to create the life you dream of.

Do The Work:

Reflection Questions:

1. How would you describe the design of your schedule?
2. Is there a central guiding purpose that governs how your schedule is designed, or does it seem that external forces have more control over it?
3. Is the design of your schedule free to evolve so that more of your time flows through that purpose?

6
THE FLOW OF TIME

The Colorado River flows some 1500 miles from its source high in the Rocky Mountains through the semi-arid American southwest to the lush wetlands of a vast delta in Mexico where it empties into the Gulf of California. As snow and glaciers melt in the Rockies each drop of water is pulled downward by gravity joining with other droplets to form small and slow rivulets that inevitably combine to form creeks and mountain streams that gain in size and flow capacity and form the headwaters of the Colorado River. As the water descends the exposed ancestral rock of the mountains, it encounters the relatively flat Colorado Plateau made up of much softer sedimentary rock that was once the bottom of the vast Western Interior Seaway. The combination of gravity and time allowed the river to carve vast canyons in its quest for the sea. During monsoon season, rain regularly falls in the otherwise dry and arid plateau. These rains can dump large volumes of water in a short period overwhelming the ground's capacity to absorb the flow. An efficient pattern emerges to channel water to join the swiftly flowing Colorado. Throughout the entire watershed, droplets which cannot be absorbed by the ground combine to form rivulets, which combine to form small streams, which combine to form creeks, which combine to form tributaries, which join the main river on its way to the sea where the pattern reverses to form the river delta.

At least this is how things worked for millions of years before humans began to assert their priorities upon the flow of the Colorado River. As humans began to flow across the landscape of the southwest, they began to alter and obstruct the flow of the river. It was small at first; some ditches to irrigate crops and small reservoirs to store the late summer rains before they disappeared down the river. A few hundred years later ditches and aqueducts started to divert the flow of The Colorado to faraway places like the opposite side of the Rocky Mountains and the large cities along the coast of southern California. Some of the largest dams on planet earth were constructed to gain more control over the flow in all seasons—permanently altering and obstructing the design of the river's flow system. As more and more people flowed into the cities of the southwest, the demand for water increased. Negotiations ensued for treaties between nations. Laws have been passed dictating usage rights between states in the southwest.

Today, every drop of water that flows in The Colorado or is stored in the vast reservoirs is carefully and strictly allocated to be diverted and used far away from the actual river. The use and diversion of the Colorado River are so extreme that water from the river no longer reaches its outlet in the

Gulf of California. The vast tree-shaped pattern of the lush river delta is disappearing. The river is no longer allowed to evolve freely and maximize access to its flow currents. All of this has obvious benefits for growth and development in these water-starved areas, yet the consequences to the natural flow system should be just as obvious. The flow system is finite, and some uses and outcomes have been given priority over the natural pattern of design created over millions of years of flowing water which had the freedom to evolve.

I'm not here to cast judgment on whether this is right or wrong. However, I do think this is a good metaphor for what can happen to the flow of our own lives.

Our time is a finite flow system. We all have the same amount. It's like the summer rains falling on the open expanses of the Colorado Plateau, it's predictable, and you probably wish there was always a little more of it. We each get 1440 minutes each day and whether you're intentionally aware of it or not those minutes get channeled into predictable patterns of flow so that you may persist in time (stay alive). At the most basic level, you and I are a finite flow system trying to persist in time. So the flow of our time gets channeled into some pretty basic patterns that provide for our survival.

A large chunk of our time gets channeled into sleep and patterns of rest. Another significant piece of time gets directed to feeding our physical bodies. That channel branches into other channels that represent time spent gathering raw materials and preparing meals so that we can eat a few times a day. Other channels of time get oriented toward output and productive contributions to the world around us.

Imagine your time is like a river basin collecting and channeling drops of water into a flowing river which eventually flows out into the ocean in the shape of a branching delta. There are routines of your life which channel a certain amount of your time inward toward things like survival, health, and personal growth. These are on the input side of the flow of time through your life. It includes eating, sleeping, exercise, education, entertainment, and a small amount of what you may do "for a living." How much or little you value these and other inputs will dictate the flow pattern which has evolved to channel your available time.

For instance, imagine someone places a high value on personal appearance. That person will have multiple predictable patterns that create channels of time around personal grooming, time at the gym, or shopping for the perfect wardrobe. All of these combine to create the personal appearance and image, which is of value to the person. Similarly, we could imagine routines and patterns for someone who values education and lifelong learning. What sort of habits and patterns would you expect from someone who places a high value on relationships and community?

All of these patterns of flow combined, go a long way toward defining who we are and what we're about as individuals. Whether through intentional thought and planning or just by accident, the way you spend your time reveals what you value and toward which purpose your life is flowing. Unlike a river, we are not solely dependent on gravity to shape and define the flow system of our lives. We are free to define our purpose and choose values that reliably feed that purpose like the main tributaries of a river. We can then thoughtfully design predictable patterns that reinforce those values. All of this assumes that you have the freedom to design the flow system of your life and can evolve when blockages occur like dams in a river. If you don't feel like you have that freedom right now, the coming chapters will help.

On the output side of the flow system are the channels of time which lead to the things we create, the outcomes we generate, the time and energy we give away, and the contributions we make to the world around us. These are priorities and goals that flow out of our purpose and often mirror the values on the input side of our flow systems. For instance, let's consider someone who places a high value on relationships and community and is also married with children. It would make sense for that person to make family a priority. We might also expect that person to design predictable patterns that reinforce that priority. That person might also create predictable patterns that help their family engage with wider communities or extended families.

That is to say; this is what we *could* expect from someone who wanted to use Constructal Law to design a flow system that channeled time through their values to live a life of purpose and gave priority to the outcomes that mattered most. Like a river delta, the output side of your life's flow system should be lush, productive, and full of life! Does this seem hopelessly idealistic to you? I assure you it's not. This is how I design and live my life, and it's how my wife and I design our family life. By using the principles of Constructal Law to develop a better flow system for your time, you'll get there too.

Obstacles and Diversions

The sad reality is that very few of us *feel* like we have the freedom to design our lives to maximize the flow of our available time toward what truly matters to us. If statistics hold, your life is a complex flow system riddled with obstacles and diversions that serve competing interests that may or may not represent what truly matters to you. Let me paint a picture as an example and see if any of it sounds familiar.

Our culture tells us to value success, including the success of our children, above all else. Success is primarily measured in terms of financial capital and status within a particular field or organization. That leads to us funneling an ever-increasing amount of time toward work and career to achieve the priority of financial success or to climb the corporate ladder. We put pressure on our kids to succeed in school and spend increasing amounts of financial capital to move into the best school districts or pay for private education.

Of course, the big fancy homes are a symbol of success as well so win-win, right? But success at school isn't enough these days, so the kids have to participate in lots of sports and extracurricular activities. More time gets funneled toward the value of success and the priority of attaining the markers of achievement. Along the way, you may have said yes to more than a few commitments that are more about the values and priorities of others than your own, but that's what it takes to get ahead, right? These tend to be like an aqueduct siphoning water from a river, easier to get started than to stop. How many diversions of your time and energy are channeling flow toward outside interests?

Our society values economic growth and depends on our contributions on both sides of the ledger book. In accounting terms, we are seen as "human capital," and every bit of our productivity and value to the workplace is tracked. You may have the very unusual privilege of having your values and priorities align well with how you spend your time at work or even with what you choose to learn. However, statistics say that a vast majority of us end up doing what is valuable to the company or organization but often holds little to no meaning at a personal level.

One reason this dissatisfaction persists is the way modern life ties income generation together with core identity. You are what you do for a living. It is easier than ever to generate income from sources that don't require a lifetime commitment, yet a life outside of the 9 to 5 career is often considered unsafe and irresponsible. Studies have shown that most workers in the modern world could easily accomplish their job requirements in less than half the standard 40-hour workweek. It's an open secret, but we don't talk about it. Whose interest does it serve to have people sitting around in cubicles wasting time? What would happen if everyone suddenly had an extra day or two to devote to their own interests, values, and priorities? More on this later. For now, ask yourself what percentage of the time you spend "working" aligns with what you care about most? I'm not suggesting that everyone should run out and quit their 9-to-5. I only want you to consider the possibility that your job might be an obstacle to the life of your dreams.

Of course, a big part of why we work so much is to increase the amount of stuff and entertainment we can consume. Our culture values economic growth, and so we must be convinced to do our part as a consumer of goods and services. Vast amounts of our economy are now oriented toward "convenience" products or services for those who have no time. What would happen if a large portion of us suddenly valued time and relationships over an excess of financial capital? What if you and everyone else didn't *need* to buy processed convenience food any longer because you had time to cook food with your family? What if some significant portion of our society decided to value experiences over things?

My point is that as a culture, we're all invested heavily in the status quo, and so vast amounts of money are devoted to marketing to normalize behavior that supports it. You're reading this book, so I'm going to go ahead and assume that you're not satisfied with the status quo. The only way to take back your time is to design a life that removes blockages and diversions that don't serve your values and priorities.

If you don't define your values, purpose, and priorities, then our culture will define them for you to channel some of your time and energy toward outside interests.

Let me mention one more substantial cultural value that may fly a bit under the radar. It may not seem like it, but the value of safety comes up in nearly every area of our lives and affects many of the decisions we make about how we spend our time. Risk is considered irresponsible and dangerous in most circumstances, and therefore it's shunned and discouraged. Why risk whatever success you've managed to achieve? Better to put in your time and wait for retirement and only then do what you're putting off until later.

It's hard to know what or how to prepare our children for the future, better to play it safe by "doing it all" even if it means sacrificing other values and priorities along the way. Don't pursue what you really want to do; choose a safe option you can tolerate. Don't travel to parts unknown; the world isn't safe. Spend incredible amounts of time and money to ensure your children never encounter an unsafe environment. Let's not even get started on the time commitment of modern "helicopter parenting"—at least some of which is now considered the standard and responsible way of raising children. Buy a home in a safe neighborhood, sure to maintain its value and insulate you from risk in every way.

I could go on and on, but you probably get the picture. Please don't misunderstand me; I am not advocating the pursuit of danger and irresponsible behavior. I merely want to raise a question. Do you value safety at all costs? Maybe other values and priorities would encourage other paths and a different design for your life. Much of what we consider necessary is heavily influenced by the marketing of industries that profit from us feeling unsafe. Maybe life isn't as risky as we're made to believe and perhaps a little carefully calibrated risk will align with our values and purpose. It's time to approach your life with more intentionality.

A busy life is normal. A busy life is safe. Designing an unbusy life means turning from the status quo and breaking cultural norms. Some will try to convince you it is unsafe. This is not a trivial journey you have chosen to embark on; courage is required.

Our lives are so full of competing values and priorities that create diversions of time large and small that we are left with nothing but small pockets of time in between.

These pockets of time seem hardly worth channeling toward other things we truly value, so we turn to distractions and entertaining ways to "kill time." Things like TV, streaming media, casual games, and of course, social media of all kinds act like dams to trap small flows of our time to serve the financial benefit of others. These products may have some usefulness, yet are made more and more addictive to collect larger and larger reservoirs of our time.

This is likely to be a big reason why you don't feel like you have enough time to accomplish everything on a daily basis. Our lives end up fragmented by competing flows of time, obstacles, and diversions. This fragmentation is so frustrating that it feels good to fire up meaningless games on our phone or scroll mindlessly through a social feed. We turn to it so often because of positive feedback loops, and at least it *feels* like our choice to spend time there. Designing your life around predictable patterns of flow and according to your values, purpose, and priorities will help you take back more of your time from the distraction industry. I'm not saying you have to give it all up entirely. After all, you'll always need something to do on the toilet!

You may resonate with all of these examples or only some. Indeed, the pattern of your life is unique. However, it's highly likely that your life is at least a little bit like the Colorado River being diverted to the point that little to nothing reaches the intended destination. After large chunks of your time are spent meeting the values and priorities of the world around you, is any left for the goals and dreams that matter most to you? What are you putting off until later in life under the assumption that you don't have time for it right now? Are you sacrificing self-care and healthy habits—because who has time for that, right?

Most of us figure it's too hard to bring order and a well-designed structure to our lives. Might as well just binge watch something on Netflix. Or maybe you don't think you have the right to a life full of purpose and designed around what matters most to you? It's easier by far to say, "I don't have time" to pursue my dreams or live into my values.

When you say "I don't have time," it shifts the responsibility. It's not your fault; it's your stinking boss's fault. We shift responsibility to others like bosses, family members, school administrators, or all the other people in this stupid traffic jam. Or we may blame "society" at large and deny we have the power to design our own life.

The truth is that everything you do, every minute you spend, every diversion or obstacle you accept in your life is a choice. You have a choice. Let that sink in. Yes, there are trade-offs to be made since we all have a finite amount of time each day. However, if your life is full of activities that don't reflect what matters most to you, it's because you choose to let it stay that way. Often this is because we fail to choose something different, but that is still a choice. I'll say it again:

> *If we don't define our values, purpose, and priorities, the world around us will do it for us and divert as much of our time and attention toward what matters to others as possible until we're left with just a dried-up riverbed.*

You do have power over your own life, yet it will be impossible to change much without a clear picture of how it should be different. The rest of this book will be devoted to developing a clear picture or vision for your future and designing the flow of your time to make that picture a reality. It starts with defining a purpose for your life. You need a clear and compelling answer to the question, *why* you get up every morning and do what you do with your time. I'll help you define values that feed your purpose and declare priorities that guide your outcomes and achievements.

Make no mistake; we must live within limits. No one has time for everything they may want to do, which is why we need a flow system designed to maximize the time spent on what we decide is most important to us. Remember if we do nothing, the 2nd Law says that chaos is likely to increase. Complexity and chaos increase without any effort at all. Which is why busyness is the status quo. It takes energy and effort to bring about simplicity and efficient design. It's happening all around us. Nature is continuously converting the energy of the sun and gravity into efficient designs that fuel life and movement. It may seem hard, but you have a choice. You really do get to decide how you spend your time. Now forgive me for reinforcing my point and rounding out this chapter with a quote from a beloved mentor, Gandalf, the grey pilgrim of Middle Earth:

> *All we have to decide is what to do with the time that is given to us.*

This is *truth*, my friends.

Do The Work:

- *Take some time and **make a list of obstacles and diversions** that keep your time from flowing to what truly matters to you.*
- *Consider how many of them feel under your control. Which ones feel out of your control?*
- *What choices would you have to make to change or eliminate them?*

7

RESTORING THE FLOW

The story of the Colorado River being divvied up for the priorities of growth and development is not unique. The story is repeated with rivers all over the globe. Almost as soon as humans began large scale projects to control and capitalize on the flow of river systems, some started raising questions and concerns. What are we giving up by obstructing and diverting these living flow systems? What value are we sacrificing for the benefit gained? Is it a good trade? Is the equation always the same? Might the value of a free-flowing river system and all that comes with it be higher in some instances? Have we accounted for the values and priorities of everyone and everything affected by the decision to build a dam or siphon large amounts of water away from the source?

As it turns out, society has been rethinking the value equation over the last few decades. Increasingly we are deciding that the value of free-flowing river systems is higher than the benefit gained by dams and diversions. In some cases, the cost of maintenance has risen to unacceptable levels; in other cases, the progress of different forms of power generation have changed the value equation. In some cases, we have placed more value on the rich diversity of wildlife and entire ecosystems that are obstructed by dams or the benefits of recreation that may be lost by over development of a waterway. Whatever the reasons, over the last 30 years, there have been more than 1355 projects to restore rivers to a natural state of flow. 2017 and 2018 were both record years by far. These projects usually involve the deconstruction of one or more dams along with artificial channels, culverts and human-made structures meant to control the flow of the river system.

One recently completed example is the restoration of the Elwha River in northwestern Washington State. It is the largest river restoration project in United States history. Two hydroelectric dams had to be carefully demolished including the Glines Canyon Dam which at 210 feet tall (64 meters), is the largest dam in the United States to be removed to restore the flow of a river system. The project took years to complete, and the river will need many years of freedom to evolve and reclaim its natural design which provides efficient channels for the flow of water from a large mountainous section of Olympic National Park to the river's mouth in the Strait of Juan de Fuca. Even though it will take a long time to entirely erase the evidence of the large reservoirs and restoration efforts, many of the intended benefits like the return of salmon to spawn in the upper Elwha have manifested in short order. I find the project fascinating, and I think it's a good object lesson in choosing specific values and restoring a flow system to support them. Let's follow the project from start to finish and see if we can't find transferable principles for our own lives.

What Is The Purpose Of The River?

Long before the decision was made to restore the Elwha, the stakeholders had to answer a fundamental question. What is the purpose of the river? Early European settlers to the Port Angeles area looked at the river and decided its primary purpose would be to provide power for commerce and the growing population arriving in the area. This purpose was in opposition to the use of the river by people native to the area as well as the river's purpose into the broader flow system, which includes plants and animals.

By making the purpose of the river about providing power, early settlers were valuing economic growth, development, and human convenience. With this framework, the decision to build dams to harness the river's purpose made a lot of sense. The river was a clean way to produce the desired outcome of power generation. It also allowed for more control over seasonal flooding, which protected development and economic investment. I'll admit this is, perhaps, a little simplistic but you can begin to see the values that fed the purpose which produced specific outcomes. It's a flow system of inputs and outputs flowing through a particular purpose. All of this is accomplished at the expense of the river's original purpose—to provide an efficient way for water to flow from high in the Olympic mountains and out into the nearshore estuary in the straits.

The river in its natural state of flow serving its original purpose is inextricably linked to many other flow systems.

The flow of adult salmon upstream and young salmon downstream. The flow of larger wildlife like bears which depend on the flow of salmon. The flow patterns of many species of birds which depend on the riparian environment provided by the river's flow system. Even the flow of sediment from erosion upstream to the estuary ecosystem at the mouth of the river. All of these flow systems were dramatically affected by the construction of dams. The dams were obstacles to the otherwise predictable pattern of design for these systems. Some flow systems were destroyed entirely. The salmon could no longer flow upstream. In other words, the finite flow system of salmon in the Elwha River could not persist in time.

Transferable Principle:

My point here is to illustrate just how important defining a purpose for the flow system known as your life is. It is central and essential to designing the life of your dreams. Purpose influences all aspects of the life you will create. It's like the main branch of a flowing river. Or, to switch metaphors, it's like the beating heart of the cardiovascular system. In the next few chapters, we will design predictable patterns to channel time into defined values that reinforce your stated purpose so you can achieve the goals and priorities that truly matter to you. It's all designed around your purpose in life, and we'll turn to that in the next chapter.

What Values Will Guide The Project?

Once the stakeholders in the Elwha River area decided to restore the river to its original purpose, they needed to decide on a set of values to guide the project moving forward. For example, they could have agreed to value speed and financial efficiency. That would have meant allowing the demolition crews a lot more freedom to use the quickest and cheapest method of removing the dams. Instead, they decided on values like low environmental impact and safety. That meant contractors had to be as careful as possible not to introduce foreign sediments into the river system. That meant taking the dams apart slowly and carefully, to remove as much of the building materials as possible from the river. It involved providing access to various scientists who could monitor and measure the impact from start to finish. It meant designing solutions to the challenging problem of taking apart a very tall dam built in a narrow canyon. It would have been much easier and faster to blow the whole thing sky high and deal with cleaning up the mess after the reservoir was gone. However, that would have violated the values of the project which were in place to serve its intended purpose.

Imagine for a moment if the stakeholders merely stated the purpose of restoring the flow of the river and told contractors to make it happen with no other guidance. The demolition contractors would bring their own set of values to the project, which would likely conflict with those of the stakeholders.

Transferable Principle:

If we don't define a set of values to reinforce our purpose, we will end up at the mercy of other interests whose values are likely to conflict with ours and will undermine our purpose. We may even find our values blocked by obstacles with reservoirs of time building up to serve the interest of others rather than our values and purpose. In chapter nine, I'll help you define a set of values that will reinforce the purpose of your life.

What Outcomes Will Be Prioritized?

Before getting started, and then continuously throughout the restoration project, specific results had to be prioritized, planned for, and progress measured. Those managing the project faced a variety of constraints. They need to consider time constraints, budget constraints, and environmental constraints. Not every desired outcome was either possible or realistic. For example, I'm sure the stakeholders would have been thrilled if there was a way to entirely erase the environmental impact of dams being in place for a century. The problem is that there was a century's worth of sediment trapped by the dams, which would all be released in a short amount of time. There is no way to rewind the clock and deposit that sediment slowly over the last 100 years. All they could do is plan for best-case scenarios and prioritize the most critical outcomes. Once those were defined, and long after the dams are removed, scientists will be monitoring the results and revising plans around plant and wildlife restoration. A few years after the last chunk of the upper dam was removed, some outcomes were quick to come while others will happen more slowly. Scientists continue to monitor the results and adjust plans to achieve the priorities set at the beginning of the project.

Transferable Principle:

To live a life full of meaning and purpose, we will need to define what outcomes and achievements are a priority to us. What contributions will we make that mirror our values and express our purpose to the world around us? What do we hope to achieve personally, both in the short-term and in the future? We have a limited amount of time and will not be able to accomplish what matters most to us if we spend time pursuing everything that catches our attention. Neither will we express our real purpose if we devote large streams of time to the priorities of others. We cannot achieve all ends, and so we must set priorities that match our values and express our purpose. However, I will promise you this, by designing your life around Constructal Law, you will achieve more than you thought possible and still *feel* like you have more time.

Survey The Current Reality

Before the restoration project can get underway in earnest, there needs to be a comprehensive and accurate survey of the entire system. How much water is currently being held by the dams? What is the strength of the dams? Are there any structural weaknesses resulting from deferred maintenance that should be considered? How much sediment is waiting to flow downstream once the dams are gone? What kind of access is needed for the equipment required? How many new native plant starts will be necessary to aid in reforestation? Are there salmon still attempting to gain access to the river every year or will they need to be reintroduced? How will the project affect the structures and developments near the mouth of the river? The list could go on and on, but it would be impossible to move forward honoring the defined values and achieving the prioritized outcomes without an accurate picture of the situation as it is.

This information is critical to deciding what needs to be removed, what needs to stay, what needs to be reinforced, and what needs to be reintroduced. Restoring the Elwha River was a complex multi-year project. The planners needed to make decisions about what order to remove the structures and when it would be possible to reintroduce plants and biodiversity. Not everything could happen all at the same time.

Transferable Principle:

In the same way, you will need to undertake a comprehensive and accurate survey of your time. Depending on the structure of your life and commitments that take time to wind down or remove, you will likely need to make a plan to implement your new design for the flow of time in your life. That plan may need to proceed in stages as obstacles are removed and time is freed to flow toward your values, purpose, and priorities. Having an accurate picture of how your time currently flows, where it is blocked or diverted will be essential.

It's essential, to be honest with yourself and proceed without beating yourself up about reality. Remember that chaos and entropy is just the natural way of things, and it will take work and effort to bring structure and order to the flow system of your life. Without gravity the river wouldn't flow to the sea; without solar energy, water wouldn't flow from the ground through the trees into the air, and without calories from food, the heart wouldn't pump blood through our circulatory system. It takes energy to create the predictable patterns of flow all around us. Designing a flow system for how we use our time is no different.

Do The Work:

To gain an accurate picture of how you currently use your time, I suggest you keep a time diary.

You can use a spreadsheet program or look for an app built for time tracking or even use a good old sheet of paper. However you choose to record the information; what you want is an accurate account of how you spend each hour of every day for the next week or two. You could break it down into 30 or 15-minute chunks of time if you want, but rounding to the nearest hour is usually good enough to work with and easy enough to follow through with.

It's usually preferable to track each hour as it passes, but it's okay to fill it in at the end of the day if you can remember accurately. Write down enough information that you'll be able to categorize the activity later. Don't worry about the why or the purpose of each activity; write it down so you can use it to make a plan when the time comes. If your weeks are reasonably regular, then one week may be enough, but it's usually helpful to capture more than a single week since our schedules can fluctuate a bit. I know this task can be intimidating, but I promise it will be helpful and will increase your chances of successfully redesigning your life. This is just part of the work and energy required to overcome the natural trend toward disorder in our world. If we want an unbusy life, we have to do the work.

8

START WITH PURPOSE

According to the Constructal Law, any flow system providing movement from one area to another area should include a large central channel with enough capacity to support the volume and flow rate dictated by the size of the entire area that it serves. In other words, a large tree will have an extensive network of roots under the earth collecting and moving water up out of the ground and into the surrounding air through its branches and leaves. The main trunk of the tree needs to provide enough flow capacity to handle the water sent by the roots and strong enough to support the branches and leaves as they move the water into the air.

In the same way, a river will need to carve a sufficient channel of flow to handle all the water sent by the streams, creeks, and tributaries until the water reaches the mouth or delta. The same is true for traffic flows of all kinds designed by everything from urban planners to theme park architects.

Our lives are no different. At the center of the flow system of your time, there needs to be a *purpose* that gives direction and guidance to your entire life. It needs to be specific to you and what motivates you at a gut level. It needs to be robust enough to stand the test of time. What makes you want to get out of bed every morning and not just today but for the rest of your life?

Purpose is that gut instinct formed by your personality and experiences. You're probably close to your purpose in those moments when you notice your heart seems to sing. It's tied to what you believe about yourself and your contribution to the world around you. The good news is that you don't need to invent your purpose because you already have one. I only need to help you give words to what is only operating at a gut level and not tied to language and reason.

Let me step back and map out the whole flow system we're designing together. Imagine all of the seemingly small everyday routines of your life. These are like the small streams and creeks that feed the tributaries of a river basin. In chapter ten, I'll teach you how to make these predictable and oriented towards feeding the flow of your time into a few main channels that we'll call your values. These values collect the flow of your everyday routines and feed it through the central purpose of your life.

On the outcomes side of the flow system, are your priorities. These are the branches of output that give guidance to your productive time and should relate to the values on the other side of your purpose. These are like the main channels of a fertile and productive river delta or the main branches of a tree that lead to the smaller fruit-bearing branches. We'll cover values and priorities in the next chapter and the productive routines that are tied to your priorities in chapter ten. This structure forms a tree-like flow system similar to that of a river and is illustrated below.

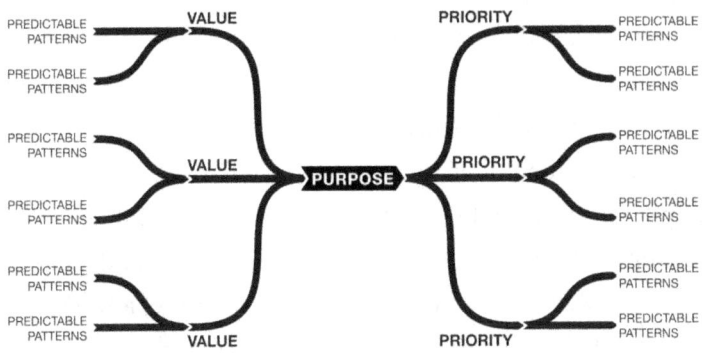

You may have more values and priorities, and that's fine, but they all need to flow through a central guiding purpose for the design of your life. The rest of this chapter is devoted to helping you uncover what that is, and putting it into a simple statement that is actionable and easy to remember. Then in the chapters to come, we'll work out from the center and get intentional about every moment of your time so that you are living a life full of purpose, on purpose.

To understand each part of the flow system, you may find it helpful to think of purpose as the answer to *why* you do the things you do, the way you do them. You could think of your values as representing *how* you do all the little things that shape who you are. You could think of your priorities as representing *what* you do that contributes something to the world around you.

So then, you could think of your purpose as

expressing *why* you do what you do and how you do it. But knowing why we do things is often not easy to put into words. Our motivations come from a deep gut level of our consciousness that has no capacity for language and speech. It's related more towards emotions and instincts than logic, reason, and language. So to give voice to this part of ourselves, we need to dig in and engage that part of our brain from a less than direct angle.

Often when asked why they do what they do directly, people will use the logical part of their brain to answer. Ask someone why they bought a particular watch, and you may get an answer like, "I needed a way to tell time, and this one was on sale." Asking why you bought the car you drive will often yield something about the excellent gas mileage and strong safety rating. Is that really why we choose a *specific* make and model? Why do you go to work every day? *For the paycheck. To pay the bills.* Really? We often turn to logical answers because we find it difficult to express the emotions behind our choices with words.

Answers like these may be valid on a particular logical level, but if we dig deeper, we could discover a more authentic sense of motivation and purpose. If we dig long enough and deep enough, we could uncover a central guiding purpose that tends to motivate much of what we do, what we buy, and how we spend our time. That is unless we've been convinced to ignore our sense of purpose in favor of other priorities like a steady paycheck, loyalty to a friend, or a sense of obligation to family.

Some of us are fortunate to have our job line up with our purpose, leading to a deep sense of fulfillment. Many are not so lucky and suffer from a lack of fulfillment in the workplace. Perhaps we said yes to an opportunity that was misaligned with the core purpose of our life, and we feel like we work only for the paycheck. Maybe we took a job at a moment when we really needed the financial capital and never looked back to question if it was the right fit in the long run.

The truth is, even if we didn't need the money, we would still need to devote a portion of our time to productive labor. Whether it's for a paycheck or not, we all need to contribute to something bigger than ourselves that expresses our purpose in life, and so we go to work. Feeling fulfilled by that labor shouldn't come down to luck. You can discover your purpose, and you can design your life around it.

In a smaller but still significant way, the watch (or phone or shoes, etc.) you choose to purchase and wear says something about your values which feed your purpose. The real trick is to design a system where all of these seemingly unrelated decisions, routines, inputs, and outputs align to flow through the central guiding purpose of your life. So let's uncover your purpose so you can get started building that system of flow for your life.

Step One: Storytelling

One of the predictable patterns of my family's life is to host a weekly family-style meal with friends and neighbors wherever we are in the world. It's an expression of our values and our purpose, and we hope the outcome is stronger relationships and families all around. Every week people gather in our home, and everyone contributes to a meal together, and for those few hours, our home becomes their home, and we all become a family. After several years of doing this no matter where we call home, we have found that with a bit of intentionality, it doesn't take long for strangers to become something like an extended family.

One of the things that happen when people gather for a meal every week is that they run out of small talk and start telling stories. We tell stories about how we met our spouses or the funny stuff our kids do. We tell stories about our hopes and dreams as well as stories about our deep frustrations in life. If you keep it up long enough, walls will start to come down, and people will begin to tell stories that reveal both who they are and who they long to be at a deep and visceral level.

I'm writing this chapter the morning after one of our "Sunset Sunday" gatherings. They are always fun, but last night was just the right mix to create something unique. A few of the families have been coming every week for months now, yet last night we added a couple of new families as well. There was just the right combination of ages, games, and a new Disney movie to keep the younger folks happy after dinner and give the adults some significant time to talk.

Chit chat gave way to storytelling, and we began to learn all sorts of information about each other. Family secrets came out because, well, we felt like we *were* a family. Hopes and dreams flowed through the stories we told about where we've been and where we're going. You see, the common thread currently is that we're all families who travel much of the time. We learned a lot about each other when someone got us telling stories about the stickiest situations we've encountered during our travels. It's not just the stories we tell but the way we tell them that matters. It's what makes us go quiet and thoughtful and what makes us belly laugh until our sides hurt. Storytelling can be a powerful window into the deepest parts of who we are.

So we will begin to uncover your purpose with stories.

I'm going to ask you to recall a collection of stories that represent peaks and valleys in your life. You'll need some method of writing them down, so grab a notebook, laptop, phone, or even a bunch of sticky notes before you move forward.

These stories don't need to be the most significant events in your life, but they do need to be meaningful in some specific way. Details are important. If it's a story about some recurring memory, find one that contains specific details about people or emotions.

For instance, I just told you a story about our meal nights but then got specific with the details of one in particular. Don't just write down a story about holidays at grandma's house. Find one specific holiday that stands out for some reason. Who made it stand out? How did you feel about it? I want you to come up with a dozen specific memories that you can tell a story about with details. So that you don't overthink it too much, I'm going to prompt you with a list of potential stories, but if something comes to mind that's not on the list, feel free to write it down.

Write down enough details about the moment so that you can tell the story later, but don't write out the whole thing just now. Pay particular attention to your emotions both in the stories, and while you recall them.

- Think about the stories you tell about yourself

over and over again. What stories do you share about your childhood, accomplishments, or even mistakes you've made? Write down the ones that seem most meaningful. Be specific about why you tell each one. Are there any details that you've fudged a bit? Are there details that you consistently leave out? This exercise is for your benefit, and it helps to be honest with yourself.

- Recall a happy memory from your childhood and note as many details as you can, including who was there at the time. What made it meaningful? Why do you think this one stands out?
- Think about people who have had a big impact on you or have influenced you in some way. What was it about them that left such a mark on your life. Note specific moments when they seemed to shape the direction of your future.
- Think about a moment from work or school when you just couldn't stop what you were doing because you were enjoying it so much or you just had to see it through to the end. What specifically kept you going?
- Can you recall a moment in life when you wondered if you could possibly go on with things the way they were? What triggered that moment? Try to dig deep and look for root causes to add to the story.
- Think about a moment when you were overwhelmed by a sense of accomplishment and pride in what you did. Note the details.
- Think about a moment when you were

overwhelmed with disappointment. Get specific about why that moment sticks out.
- If you had to pick only two or three highlights of your life, what would they be? What is it about those moments that make them stick out more than others?
- When you were a child, what did you say you wanted to be when you grew up? How and why did that change as you grew older? Try to remember specific moments when the answer changed and why.
- Feel free to repeat as many of these as you like until you have around 12 solid stories you can tell.

Once you have your collection of stories, you need to start sorting through them for meaning hidden just below the surface. The path forward will depend a bit on how you process information best. Some people, like my wife, are internal processors. People wired this way are much better at analyzing data and experiences and reaching decisions about life if given adequate time to reflect on their own. If this is the way you're wired up, I think you could benefit from devoting a few hours to journaling these stories. Take some time to fill in the details and challenge yourself to look for critical facts and relevant details while you're writing. Start collecting those facts and distilled meanings somewhere. Don't overthink it; if it feels like it might be important at all then write it down for later.

If you're like me and the idea of sitting alone and writing out all of these stories sounds like torture to you, then you are probably a verbal processor. You are going to need some help. I recommend you seek out a partner who can help you by actively listening and jotting a few notes while you tell your stories. Give them permission to ask questions that will help you pull out more details as you tell the stories. Ask your partner to jot notes about key facts and important details as you tell the stories. I know this might seem like a barrier to moving forward, but it will be worth it. Given how we're wired up, you and I will have a tough time trying to process the useful bits of information out of these stories without communicating them verbally.

Either path you take should yield a page or two of notes filled with key facts and meaningful details that you'll need to move forward. Don't shortcut the process. Make time to do the work; I promise it's worthwhile!

Step Two: Common Threads

Once you have your notes from step one, it's time to start sorting and sifting. What you're looking for are the common threads and themes that seem to come up more than once. Look for ideas, words, and emotions that seem to recur in your stories. Don't discount a theme that might manifest itself in both positive and negative ways in your stories. Don't stop at just a few, keep digging and sifting until you've uncovered at least five. If you worked with a partner on step one, it could be beneficial to ask them to help you with this step as well. If you worked alone on step one and you find it challenging to connect the dots, consider if it might be helpful to ask for help from someone you trust. Once you've had the chance to process your stories internally, it can be helpful to have another perspective when trying to identify the common threads.

For example, when I gathered and told my stories, many of them involved the common thread of gathering friends together for many reasons. As early as I can remember, my house was where neighborhood kids would gravitate for a game of tag or dodgeball or squirt gun wars. I would often go around the block knocking on doors to see if kids could come over for a neighborhood game. When my wife and I were newly married and still in college, we regularly lured our friends over with food and fun. The thread continues to this day and was easy to spot when I was done telling stories.

More than a few of my stories involved the common thread of being out in the natural world; from family vacations to Yellowstone and the shores of Lake Michigan to more recent experiences hiking through the sequoias or to the bottom of the Grand Canyon. Feeling a connection to the natural world is a thread that runs from my childhood to today.

Perhaps my strongest emotions are tied to a desire to find freedom from the status quo that so quickly fills our lives with obstacles and distractions. Some of the stories I told about my childhood involved severe acts of what you might call "misbehavior." However, at the core of most of my childhood misadventures, is a rebellion against a controlling influence. I may have lacked the maturity to sort through what was worth adapting to and how to object to systems of control in responsible ways, but the strong desire to get free was there very early on. Much of my adult life has been about finding healthy ways to identify and rebel against the constant pressure to adapt to external values and priorities.

Other themes from my stories included a strong preference for new ideas and a desire to simplify life in a wide variety of ways.

Once you have identified several themes from your stories, it's time to narrow the list down. Go ahead and circle one or two that seem to overshadow the rest. Ask yourself which one would you share if you had to choose one to share with others in a short bio, which one makes you say, YES!? That's what I'm all about. If you have a hard time narrowing it down to just one, go with your gut. Pick one and test it out in the next step. If you get to the end and it doesn't feel right, you can easily pick the other one and try again. Hold on to all of the themes you've identified and keep them handy. They will likely indicate some of your values and priorities.

Step Three: Statement of Purpose

Now it's time to craft a statement of purpose. We'll use that one theme that seems to speak with more volume and clarity than the rest. Your purpose needs to be specific to you and your contribution to the world, but also help you make decisions about the design of your life. So think about the theme you've chosen and ask yourself what contribution would seem to flow out of it if you were to apply it to helping others. What impact is that theme likely to have on others around you if you make it the central organizing principle of your life?

Your purpose is the main trunk of the flow system of your life and should be oriented toward flowing "downstream." Your time will flow through predictable patterns and rhythms of life through your values and into your purpose where the transition moves toward flowing out into the contributions you make to the world around you. It's helpful then if your purpose is "outward" facing since it will help keep things flowing in the right direction.

For example, freedom from external control is the most substantial theme in my life. At times in my youth, I let that flow the wrong direction, and it manifested in selfish and unhealthy ways. However, if I let my values create a life of freedom, I am free to help others get free as well. So this is the first half of my purpose, *to help people get free*. That can't be it though, because it's just too vague without some vision for the impact this will have in the world. What does it mean to get free? Is it my idea of freedom that I should force on everyone I meet? Painful experience has taught me that leads in an unhelpful direction.

So I need to pair it with an idea of the impact my contribution will make. What do I really want for myself and others? I want everyone to be free to design and live the life of their dreams. So my purpose is **to help people get free *so that* they can build the life of their dreams**. That second half gives guidance to my gut-level instinct to seek freedom for myself and others by reminding me that *my* dreams are not universal. I want to help everyone find the freedom to build the life they dream about. That is my purpose. Having language to express what is a mostly gut-level motivation inside us can help us maintain a healthy orientation and make better decisions about how to design the flow of our time.

All of this suggests a bit of a formula for how to word your statement of purpose:

The Formula:

To {your contribution} **so that** {the impact it makes on the world}

My Example:

To {help people get free} **so that** {they can build the life of their dreams}

This formula is just a helpful structure for how to word your purpose. You can stray away from this formula in the end, but it's useful if you can fit it into this wording at first to make sure that it is both outward-facing and results in some specific impact on the world around you.

This statement should be robust and durable. It should have enough flow capacity to channel every minute of every day. It should also be durable enough to stand the test of time. If it doesn't feel like you've come up with something that would have been helpful a decade ago and will still be useful a decade from now, then take a step back and keep trying.

Here are a few other examples of purpose statements from people I've coached that might help you get a feel for what you're after:

- **To** create space for people to gather **so that** they can become part of the family.
- **To** shed light on what's possible **so that** we can create great things together.

- **To** connect deeply with people **so that** we can build community together.
- **To** empower and educate people everywhere **so that** they can improve their lives and achieve their goals.

Don't give in to the temptation to make this statement somehow fit with the current state of your life, job, and schedule. We are searching for something true about you. We are not trying to change you to fit the values and priorities of others. I want to help you design your life to match what is true about you. Be honest with yourself, and we'll worry about the consequences in a later chapter. No matter what the world says about what your contribution should be, use this space to declare what your true purpose is and how you imagine the impact of that purpose in the world.

It may take a while before you get the wording just right and that's okay. However, don't wait to move on until you have it perfect. Again we're trying to give words to something at the gut level, and that's hard work. Even if it's rough at first, get something down and start testing it out on people who know you well. Ask them if it sounds right and listen to their feedback. The word "build" wasn't in my original draft. I had written that the impact would be people "living" the life of their dreams. Someone suggested I insert the word build since it fits well with my background in design and construction and the reality that it takes work to live that life. I immediately added it in, and I think it's much better at expressing what I'm all about.

Once you have something close enough and you feel good about moving forward with, it's time to start designing the tributaries that will flow into and out of this central purpose of your life.

Do The Work

Most of this chapter is about doing the work, so I'll use this space to encourage you to pause in your reading and actually work through this chapter to discover your purpose if you haven't already. I know it's hard and it'll take time, but we can do hard things! I believe hard things *inspire* us.

If you've done the work and have your purpose written down, I encourage you to commit it to memory. It needs to begin carving a channel in your life like that of a river cutting through layers of sediment. Memorizing your purpose is one of the best ways to start the process.

9

VALUES AND PRIORITIES

Another predictable pattern of designs in nature, according to Constructal Law, is balance. There is always a balance between what flows into and out of a flow system. Consider the design of a tree. While the design of the root system is not identical to the design of the branches and leaves, there is a direct relationship between the two parts of the system. As the root system grows and develops more capacity for moving water up from the earth, so too must the branches and leaves grow to handle the increased flow of water on its way to the atmosphere. There is a balance between the inputs and outputs of the flow system.

This balance is everywhere if you look around a bit. River delta or estuary systems will evolve in harmony with the capacity of the entire river basin. There is a balance in our respiratory system; for every breath in, there must be a breath out. There is a balance similar to a mirror image to your body's vascular system. The blood vessels that carry oxygenated blood from the heart and lungs to our cells are mirrored by those that carry the spent blood back to the center of the system. A well-designed airport will balance the flow of passengers arriving and departing.

Significant problems arise when this balance is disrupted or ignored. Traffic jams are inevitable if highways are constructed and enlarged with an ever-increasing capacity to collect traffic with little to no increase in capacity for that traffic to flow off the highway, in or near the city. The flow system is desperately out of balance. Blockages in our cardiovascular system make our heart work much harder to maintain balance on both sides of the flow system. If a construction project dramatically alters and disrupts the root system of a tree, there will be consequences to the visible part of the flow system as well (if it survives at all).

Think back to the blockages in our flow of time created by the entertainment and social media industries. They can encourage a lack of balance between the input flow and output flow of our lives, leaving us with the feeling that we haven't accomplished as much as we wanted to. It leaves a lingering sense that our lives are out of balance.

The same can be true when we devote larger and larger amounts of time to productivity. Our time is a finite flow system, and an imbalance between inputs and outputs is inevitable at some point. Eventually, the whole system will react negatively to the imbalance.

With all of this in mind, I want to give language to the input side and output side of our lives that will help us design a life of balance. Up until now, I've resisted using the words "rest" and "work" because their definition in our culture can be overly narrow. However, I would like to be able to use them in a broad sense to talk about flows of time that feed our capacity and flows that drain our capacity. Think of a river system, there is a tree-like design structure that feeds capacity into the main river, and at the other end, there is a tree-like structure that drains the river of its flow capacity.

I would like us to think about *rest* as that side of our time-based flow system that feeds our capacity. That includes any activity that *restores* your capacity. Time spent eating, learning, recreating, and hanging out with friends would all fall on the **rest** side of the flow system. So would things related to self-care like exercise, meditation, grooming, hygiene, and visits to the doctor. Exercise might seem like work, but it is building and restoring your physical capacity, so it belongs on the rest or input side of the flow system of our time.

Because the universe is full of resistance, we need to give shape and structure to our lives so that there is adequate access to a flow of time that feeds our capacity to live out our purpose. To that end, we will designate 3 to 5 main channels to serve as conduits of our time on the input or rest side of the system. These are your *values*, and they give language to how you live your life and grow your capacity to contribute to the world around you.

I would like us to think about *work* as that side of the flow system that directs our capacity to the productive contributions we make to the world around us. That, of course, includes your time devoted to income generation. For most this will be "full-time" employment, be it a corporate or professional career or even self-employment. However, for an increasing amount of people, this may be something less than a full-time collection of efforts resulting in multiple income streams, both active and passive. That may incorporate work in the "gig economy" or internet-based passive income. This collection may also include "work" that generates returns in other forms of currency like intellectual, relational, or even spiritual capital.

For instance, I have created a few passive income streams over the past several years that generate a significant portion of the income my family needs every month. This allows me to devote a more substantial amount of time to what I consider my vocation of helping people to get free and build the life of their dreams. Some of the time I devote toward living my purpose generates income (coaching business leaders), and some create other forms of capital. For instance, I consider personal fulfillment and relationships to be more valuable forms of capital than dollars.

However, when I first started using the principles outlined in this book to design the flow of my time, I had a very different equation on the income generation and output side of my flow system. I worked half-time in the non-profit sector and as a freelance creative for the other half. I had a lot of freedom over the details of my schedule but still had to "clock-in" for well over 40 hours every week. I think a more predictable 9 to 5 work life would have made it easier for me to start designing my life around Constructal Law and predictable patterns. It took an incredible amount of work, intentionality, and self-discipline to move from plan to action. It doesn't matter if you work a traditional 9 to 5 or in the freelance gig economy. This process and the resulting design for your life will work either way and pay considerable dividends in more than just financial capital.

My point is that whether or not I currently earn money from an activity, it's still all on the work side of the flow system of my life. In this way, I feel free to live out my purpose and priorities in life, whether they generate financial capital or not. I have designed my life to ensure that I produce other forms of wealth like intellectual, physical, and relational capital.

It's important to note that this is a result of almost a decade of progress. It wasn't always this way for me. It's the life I dreamed of, and I designed my life to make my dreams a reality. I have a good deal of financial freedom because of how I designed my life, not the other way around.

To be clear, it is not because of some pre-existing financial freedom that I was able to design the life of my dreams.

For instance, I'm sure that many will assume that we can travel full-time because we have a certain amount of wealth or income that makes it possible. In reality, our method of traveling full-time allows us to live on less financial capital and income than when we owned a house in Michigan and lived a relatively typical middle-class life in America.

Please don't miss this essential fact: *I'm describing my dream.* I'm expressing my idea of freedom. It took years of designing and tweaking and increasing capacity in all areas of my life to make this dream a reality. It took years of simplifying and bringing order to the flow system of my life to make it the life I currently live. I hope my journey and success is inspiring, but it's only one example of how the freedom to live an unbusy life can look.

Others may find freedom in a regular, predictable

paycheck from a full-time career that is well-aligned with their purpose, values, and priorities. That is great, and I have coached many people to optimize their life around that work to bring balance to both the rest and the work side of their flow system. I've watched them declare their purpose boldly, which helps them make sure that their work continues to be well-aligned with their values and priorities long into the future.

However, some people I coach express that they feel trapped in a full-time job that doesn't align with their purpose, values, and priorities. If that is true of you, I hope you'll at least consider that there are other ways to design your life. Accepting a full-time career as inescapable can often lead to what environmental scientists call mismatched conditions. This can occur when we've given over large amounts of our time to an environment that doesn't fit with our purpose, values, and priorities and we'll talk more about it in the last chapter of the book.

Other activities on the work side of the system include time spent helping others and all the things large and small that we consider "chores" but really help keep the rest of our life flowing. Generative hobbies like art, crafts, music, woodworking, and the like can count on both sides. So too can time spent making space for a relaxing activity. For instance, consider the meal that our family hosts every week. It takes a good deal of work from every member of our family to make it happen. Once everyone has arrived and we're enjoying our time together, we may be over in rest territory, but it took a few hours of work to make it happen.

As a reflection of your values, you'll designate 3 to 5 main channels to direct the work side of your flow system which we'll call *priorities*. There is no end to the amount of time we could devote to the work side of our lives and no shortage of outside influences trying to divert your time to their priorities. Defining priorities that reflect your values and express your purpose in the work that you put out into the world is essential to designing the life of your dreams.

We'll start by defining your values because your priorities should be a reflection of your values and not the other way around. You can't give away what you haven't first received. The seed which eventually becomes a tree must first put down roots. Every flow system begins on the input side of things. We must work from a place of rest, not rest from our work. It's the law. Umm, it's the Constructal Law of physics, that is.

Define Your Values

The first thing I want to say about both your values and your priorities is that these should be things that are *already* true about you. They should express how you live and what you do when you are true to your motivations and what fills your life with meaning. You may be living in part or wholly according to the values and priorities of others, but you already have ways of living and working that bring fulfillment, and we're going to uncover those ways so you can design a life around them.

In other words, your values should *not* be **aspirational**. They should *not* be things you wish were true or an expression of how you think others want you to be wired up. We should all seek to change and grow over time, and you may *express* your values differently in the future. For now, be honest with yourself in defining values that are true and let them evolve over time as you grow. We're looking for what seems "normal" to you when you're at your best.

Here's the good news, you've already done a lot of the work necessary to uncover your values! Grab your notebook or whatever you used to make your list of themes from the stories you gathered in the last chapter. The ones left over that didn't become your statement of purpose are a list of behaviors, moments, and ideas that are truly important to you.

You should have a list of 5 or more themes, and we're going to whittle them down to 3 to 5. Why 3 to 5? Well, the metaphor of a river system has proven helpful over time when applying the Constructal Law to the flow system of our time. Constructal Law says that every branch of a river system should have four tributaries flowing into it before those start branching off themselves. However, in a natural world full of resistance, the real number of branching tributaries is *usually* four but sometimes three and sometimes five. In my experience of helping people to define values, three seems to be a little limiting, though on a few occasions with particular circumstances, it felt just right. The most common number of values seems to be four, with plenty of people (like me) ending up with five. There is no right or wrong answer. All I can recommend is to shoot for four and if it feels right to have one more or one less, then go for it!

The easiest way to narrow your list down is to look for themes that are either duplicates or a similar way of expressing the same idea. Find a way to combine them or simply cross one out if you like one of the versions better. If that gets you to 4 or 5 then great, you're ready to move on. If not, then you need to go with your gut. Which four (give or take one) seem to genuinely express how you truly act and behave when you're at your best? Go ahead and circle them. Easy right? Well, easier than the last chapter anyway!

As an example, let me share my list of themes that came out of telling my stories:

- Community
- Simplicity
- Sensitive to balanced rhythms and lack thereof
- Seek inspiration
- Open to change
- Love the beauty of nature
- Happier with less "stuff"
- Family relationships

These are what was left after I crossed off a couple that had to do directly with my purpose of seeking freedom. You'll notice a couple in there that relate to each other like simplicity and wanting less stuff, but they seemed to stand on their own, so I left them in. I don't know what your list looks like exactly, but I've done this enough times to know that most people end up with something like mine. That is to say a list of relatively abstract themes. Community may be something I care about but what I really need is a statement that is more action-oriented. After all, we want these values to guide what we *do* with our time. So after we do a bit of initial pruning, we need to find a way to express our values so that they guide our actions and behaviors.

Sticking with my example, let's move through the process to give you a clearer picture. Right off the bat, I saw some similar themes, and that's how I narrowed my list down. Family is just a little more specific part or subsection of my community, so I moved them together. I knew that neither of those themes adequately expressed action, so I just jammed them together in preparation for the next step. Being happier with less stuff just came from a more specific and meaningful story about a chain of events inspired by giving up my personal vehicle in favor of public transit for a season. It was still about a simpler life, so I just crossed that out and kept simplicity. After I decided to combine my love for the beauty of nature with seeking inspiration, I had it down to five. Honestly, that feels about right for me, so I didn't overthink it and moved on.

Once I had it down to those five, I had to do some work to translate the themes into action-oriented statements. For instance, saying I value community is fine but just a little too vague. I want a value statement that reminds me that my behavior matters. So instead, I wrote, "do life together." Is it possible (or even healthy) to do every moment of my life with someone else? No. I merely want to remind myself that I'm at my best when I include my family or my wider tribe when at all possible. And to make it a reality that borders on autopilot, I have defined predictable patterns (next chapter) that become my habits and routines so that I am successful at "doing life together." Out of my original list of themes, *seek inspiration* was the only one that seemed to express a value in an action-oriented way adequately, but the rest had to change. Here's the final five:

- Community and family became: **Do life together**
- **Seek inspiration** also includes my love of nature

- Open to change became: **Embrace new ideas**
- Simplicity and less stuff became: **Keep it simple**
- Balanced rhythms became: **Obey the rhythms of life**

I share these not so they can be copied, they are specific to me and my life. Although plenty of us will have similar values to each other. They are not perfect, and they have evolved slightly over time. After all, I value embracing new ideas! The critical point is that they express what is true of how I live life when I'm happy and fulfilled. Also, I find them helpful (as is) to give shape and structure to the input or "rest" side of the flow system of my life. Don't be afraid to move forward with a list of values that is *good enough* and give yourself the freedom to tweak them over time. Often the only way to make something better is to live with it, use it, and then iterate improvements over time. If you lean towards the perfectionist side of things, try hard to move forward with something helpful and then perfect it over time.

Define Your Priorities

Your values, along with their attached predictable patterns which you'll create in the next chapter, serve to gather your available time and channel it into the capacity to live out your purpose. From there, you need to define priorities that will express your values in the productive work you do, all through the lens of your purpose. Your priorities should be a reflection of your values, just expressed in a more generative action statement. They should communicate how you make your values tangible as you work and contribute to the lives of others.

Why this outward focus on how your work impacts the lives of others? Because this is the path to fulfillment. Study after study has found that we are inwardly fulfilled as we contribute outwardly to the lives of those around us. Inversely, if we focus our time and energy only on a purpose and priorities with an inward focus, we end up living unfulfilled and self-centered lives. That does not mean that you should put the preferences of others before your own or that you should be a doormat. On the contrary, it means the best way to stand up for your happiness and fulfillment is to direct your time and energy in a positive and outward direction that aligns with *your* purpose and priorities.

Your values define **how** you build capacity and your priorities express **what** you create, produce, and contribute to the world around you. Your purpose gives voice to **why** you do it all.

Maybe read that last paragraph a couple of times.

The way forward then is *through* your values and your purpose. For each value, ask yourself, what things would I create or contribute to the world as a result of the capacity created by this value flowing through my purpose in life? For example, if I am full of inspiration because it's one of my values and my purpose is to help people get free so that they can build the life of their dreams, then one of my priorities should be to "give it away." I don't just seek inspiration for myself; I have to make giving it away to help others get free and build their dreams, a real priority in my life.

If you go through each of your values in this way, you should end up with something like my list of values and priorities:

Values >> Priorities

Do life together >> Create predictable space for community

Seek inspiration >> Give it away

Embrace new ideas >> Evaluate and evolve

Keep it simple >> Fight entropy (do the work to simplify)

Obey the rhythm of life >> Seek balanced outcomes

Again, this is my imperfect list, and yet I find it incredibly helpful such as it is. I find the phrase "create predictable space for community" to be slightly cumbersome and not as memorable as some of the others, but I just haven't found another way to say it that is both as helpful and more memorable. Do reach out and let me know if you have a better idea, and I'll keep working on it in the meantime. The phrase "fight entropy" is filled with meaning for me and is plenty specific to be helpful. The part in parentheses isn't necessary for me personally but can be beneficial when I share my list with others.

Find your own balance between statements that are specific enough to be full of meaning and yet compact enough to be memorable. One more note, it may not be immediately apparent how the phrase "evaluate and evolve" expresses my contribution to the world around me. The way I see it, the value "embrace new ideas" is all about becoming better and better at living out my purpose, and the best thing I can do for others is to use those new ideas to evaluate how I'm doing and evolve so I'm continually improving at *helping others get free so that they can build the life of their dreams.*

Remember, you're looking for an expression of what is already true of you and not how you wish you were wired up. The world is much better off if you live out what is authentic about you *at your best,* and so are you individually. I like how Howard Thurman put it:

> *Don't ask what the world needs. Ask what makes you come alive, and go do it. Because what the world needs is people who have come alive.*

Don't give in to the temptation to reinvent yourself according to what the world is asking you to be.

The truth is that our values and purpose have a shadow side that pops up when we're at our worst. The point of this book is to help you design a life that will predictably enable you to live at your best. Don't let the moments when you're not at your best lead to discouragement and a desire to live someone else's life. That is not the solution and will never lead to a life of fulfillment and meaning where you consistently contribute your best "work" to the world.

Once you have your purpose, values, and priorities defined, it can be helpful to test them out with people who know you well. Grab a person or two whom you trust and after explaining what you're trying to do, ask them to consider how well your purpose statement, values, and priorities describe what they know to be true of you at your best. Be careful though, as it's quite common for even the people closest to you not to know everything about what makes you tick. Hear them out, listen to their questions and feedback, and consider how it might help make things better. I found it helpful to refine things a bit with help from a few people who know me well as do those who I coach through the process regularly.

Now that you have the core of your flow system defined along with the main tributaries giving shape and structure to both the rest and work side of the system, it's time to attach the small creeks and streams that will collect the everyday schedule of your life and channel it through your values, purpose, and priorities.

Do The Work

Again, this chapter is mostly about doing the work, and I encourage you to take the time to define your values and priorities before moving on to the next chapter.

Once you have them defined and you've tested them out a bit, go ahead and make your system map that looks like this:

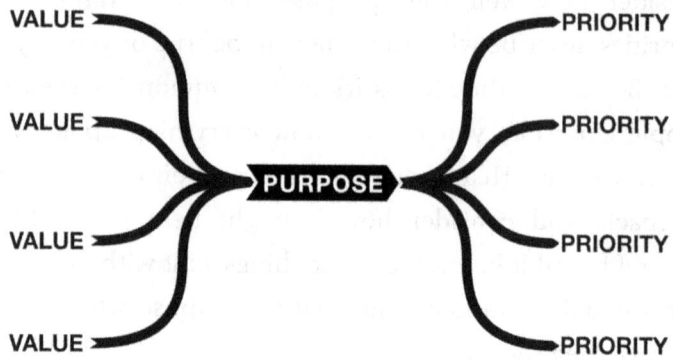

10

GET PREDICTABLE

In fiction, we find the predictable boring. In real life, we find the unpredictable terrifying. - Mokokoma Mokhonoana

Imagine the life of an early solo hunter-gatherer. Will a predator kill you in your sleep? Hard to say, but maybe not? Will you catch and kill something to eat today? Hope so. Will the next human you meet freak out and try to kill you or want to work together for food and protection? Not sure. Will it rain tomorrow? We're still working on that today, so who knows? For the solo hunter-gatherer, life was relatively uncertain and hard to predict. They may have had a *few* advantages over our work-a-day existence today, but I don't want to go back to that level of unpredictability.

The word predictable gets a bad rap. I know because I spent a large portion of my adult life terrified of being labeled as "predictable" and rejecting as many routines as I could get away with. However, the truth is that being able to predict some outcomes for ourselves is why we design everything, from our homes to user interfaces, and it's a key ingredient to happiness. You may be wired up to desire an organized and predictable life, in which case I'll talk to you later about making room for serendipity. For the rest of us who naturally want to resist predictability, we need to learn to not throw the baby out with the bathwater. Let me illustrate a bit.

For nearly a decade, my family lived in a very walkable neighborhood of a medium-sized city in the state of Michigan. On our street, the city came to collect the trash every Thursday morning. It was easy to remember, and it was just part of my routine to put our trash bin out by the curb on Wednesday evenings. Now, every *other* Thursday they would collect the recycling as well as trash. For some reason, this schedule just wasn't predictable enough. I could never remember from week to week if it was the recycling week or not. Sometimes a holiday would throw the whole thing off as well. I longed for the city to just collect it every week!

Another example comes to mind about transit schedules. Even though we had a family vehicle, I chose to depend on a combination of my bicycle and the bus system to get around the parts of town where I couldn't walk. We even chose our house in part because it was at the intersection of 3 useful bus routes. Two of those routes ran on time just like clockwork. They were predictable enough for me to count on them even if I was using them to get to a meeting on time. The other route ran through a section of town where traffic could get bad seemingly at random. I could never count on that route running on time. The unpredictability meant that if I needed to get somewhere served by that bus route at a specific time, I would have to take an earlier bus or I'd ride my bike if at all possible.

You and I may take it for granted, but we depend on the predictability of many systems in our daily lives. Can you predict what will happen when you turn on a light switch or plug something into an outlet? Not everyone in our world can. Or, imagine if every so often, when you flushed the toilet, everything went in reverse, and the sewage spewed out—you know, just to keep things interesting! I'm sure glad the result of that particular routine is predictable.

The reality is, no matter how you happen to be wired up, much of your life is predictable, and that is not a bad thing. According to research on the subject, somewhere around half of our daily actions are based purely on habits or routines that we repeat regularly. You may not even be aware of just how predictable these routines are. Yet they control all of the little mindless actions of your daily life so that your brain has time and capacity to think about other things. Imagine if you had to decide how to brush your teeth all over again every day? Imagine if you had to concentrate on every step you take, all day, every day. There wouldn't be much capacity left over.

Oceans of ink have been spent producing volumes and volumes about the power of habits over our lives—many offering hope for changing these habits and thus dramatically changing your life. However, I'm not aware of any that take a step back from these little routines of our lives and ask how they all fit into the *whole design* of our lives. How did the habits we tend to take for granted become part of our lives, to begin with? Do they fit our values, purpose, and priorities—or someone else's? Do your habits reliably channel your time to the things that truly matter to you? Or do they represent distractions, obstacles, and diversions?

Predictable Patterns

Some habits, like how you walk and brush your teeth, can be safely left as is. However, I'm willing to bet that if you look back at your time diary, you'll find more than a few routines and habits that don't fit well with the life you've designed in the last couple of chapters.

This chapter is all about getting rid of what needs to go and designing a new set of habits and routines that predictably channel your time to your values, purpose, and priorities. I call these intentionally designed routines, **predictable patterns**. These are the small rivulets and streams of time that make sure we will end up with the life we dream of, predictably. By designing predictable patterns that support your values and priorities, you will live a life of purpose, *on purpose*.

Predictable patterns can be things that occur daily, weekly, monthly, or annually. You will need predictable patterns attached to both your values and your priorities, and it's possible for one to be both "rest" and "work" at the same time. For example, an afternoon spent in the woodshop every week might be restorative or even therapeutic for you, but you'll also produce something tangible, so put that on both sides of the flow system. Here are some examples of *capacity building* predictable patterns from my own life.

Daily predictable patterns:

- I eat breakfast with my family every day. If one of us has to head out the door early then, we all get up early so we can eat together. This feeds my value to *do life together*.
- Every day before breakfast, while I drink my first cup of coffee, I read whatever Jason posted on Kottke.org the previous day. I don't have a lot of time devoted *daily* to looking for *new ideas* (one of my values). Jason's site is just the right mix of content, and I almost always find a new idea or a new angle on something that I flag for more thoughtful reading when I have more time set aside for *embracing new ideas or seeking inspiration*.
- Sleep is a predictable pattern for me. There was a time when I would follow an inspiration rabbit hole or work "in the zone" late into the night because I told myself it produced better results. Eventually, I kept track before and after embracing a regular sleep schedule. By any and every metric, I function better with proper sleep. Go figure. This is part of my value to *obey the rhythm of life* now.

Weekly predictable patterns:

- My wife and I have a date night every week. I usually file this under the value of *doing life*

together, but it also contributes to *seek inspiration* because my wife is a fantastic person who brings out the best in me.
- We host a meal night at our home every week *(do life together)*. We also have more than a few strategies which make it as easy as possible to pull off *(keep it simple)*.
- I have a decent chunk of "unstructured" time every week. It's on my weekly schedule, and I try to protect it by not scheduling meetings or other activities ahead of time. Because I have embraced structure for my life as a whole, I'm able to be utterly spontaneous about this time and not be overcome with worry about whether everything else that matters to me will get the time it needs. This time could get used for building capacity around any value and often is determined by the capacity necessary to accomplish whatever specific goal or dream toward which I'm currently working.

Monthly predictable patterns:

- I devote a day every month to *seeking inspiration* and *embracing new ideas*. It's not as essential to narrowly define the content of monthly patterns (walk in the woods, reading books, researching). What matters most is that the time is reliably and predictably set aside. The truth is that this is also mostly *unstructured* time.

Knowing that my life is well designed to attend to everything that matters to me, allows me to relax during these days and seek inspiration and new ideas.
- I have a monthly coaching call with other coaches. It's an opportunity to encourage and learn from each other *(do life together)*. It's also an opportunity to learn new ideas and best practices *(embrace new ideas)*.

Annual predictable patterns:

- For 22 years of marriage, my wife and I have taken a week-long trip for our anniversary. It's probably my longest-running intentional, predictable pattern, and it checks pretty much every box on the values side of my life.
- More recently, our family has decided to make the Family Adventure Summit (an annual event for traveling families) a predictable pattern in our life. It checks most of the boxes as well.
- I use the end of the year as a trigger for a predictable pattern of checking in on my values, purpose, and priorities. I look backward and forward. I evaluate all of my predictable patterns and decide if any need to evolve. This process is comprehensive to the entire flow system of my life, yet it is mostly about building capacity for the future.

I have other predictable patterns, but this should give you an idea of what I'm talking about. Also, I want to draw attention to the fact that you can still be spontaneous and embrace predictable patterns in your life. In fact, if you're naturally wired up to appreciate unstructured time, then the best thing you can do is *design* your life to include large chunks of it and be protective of it. Otherwise, the world will toss obstacles and distractions in your direction until you're left with a life full of structure imposed by an outside influence.

Now it's your turn.

Define your predictable patterns

Remember the Elwha River project from chapter six? I want to remind you that the planners of that project (and any major project like it) had to present a detailed vision for what *could be* before they moved forward. We'll get to the comprehensive survey of your current reality that is your time diary soon, but first, we need to spend a little more time developing your vision for what *could be*. It's time to fill in the smaller details that will make up a new framework designed to help you live the life you've always wanted. So don't worry about what your schedule currently looks like as you begin to define your predictable patterns. Once you've got that inspiring vision for the life you want, we'll go ahead and plot the route from where you are to where you want to be.

For every value and priority you've defined as part of

your flow system, come up with one daily or weekly predictable pattern as well as one monthly or annual predictable pattern. The point is to design activities that will become habits and routines that help you practice living into your values, purpose, and priorities. These predictable patterns will create pathways and channels for time to flow to what matters most to you. Once these flow patterns are defined and practiced, they will help channel the flow of your time without you having to always think about it.

The same predictable pattern can channel time into more than one value or priority, attach it to each place it feeds into. For instance, our family meal night is a predictable pattern that feeds my value of doing life together, but it's also an outcome of our priority to create predictable space for community. Other patterns like reading kottke.org every morning are only attached to the value/rest side of things while my coaching practice is a predictable pattern attached to the priority of "give it away." I have a monthly predictable pattern that is attached to three priorities (evaluate and evolve, fight entropy, and seek balanced outcomes). It's a chunk of time I devote to checking in on outcomes for all three of those priorities. In some ways, you could look at it like three separate predictable patterns which I've chosen to "batch" together, a practice which I highly recommend.

Take your time but don't overthink it too much as these will not be written in stone. Remember, part of the Constructal Law is that flow systems must have the freedom to evolve their structure to provide better and better access to their currents. These predictable patterns should be put in place as long as they provide good access for time to flow into your values and out of your priorities, but if circumstances change, you should feel the freedom to change your patterns as well. I'll talk more about staying flexible and flowing around obstacles in chapter 12.

Also, don't hesitate to give new meaning to a habit or routine that you already have. If you have a predictable pattern already in your life that fits your design well as is or with only minor changes, then use it! Most of us have habits and routines that express our values, purpose, and priorities. We may not have been able to express why we do those things with clarity, but now you can. Seeing how that predictable pattern fits with the whole design of your life can give it new meaning and make it that much more fulfilling.

Do The Work

For every **value** and **priority** you defined in the last chapter, determine one daily or weekly and one monthly or annual predictable pattern. It can be helpful to list your values and priorities and leave space for the predictable patterns like this:

Value One:

- *Predictable pattern (daily or weekly)*
- *Predictable pattern (monthly or annual)*

Value Two:

- Predictable pattern (daily or weekly)
- Predictable pattern (monthly or annual)

Value Three:

- Predictable pattern (daily or weekly)
- Predictable pattern (monthly or annual)

Priority One:

- Predictable pattern (daily or weekly)
- Predictable pattern (monthly or annual)

Priority Two:

- Predictable pattern (daily or weekly)
- Predictable pattern (monthly or annual)

Priority Three:

- Predictable pattern (daily or weekly)
- Predictable pattern (monthly or annual)

** *Remember that it's okay for one predictable pattern to serve more than one value or priority. Simply write it down wherever it applies.*

Once you have at least a couple of predictable patterns attached to each value and priority, add them to your visual flow system map like this:

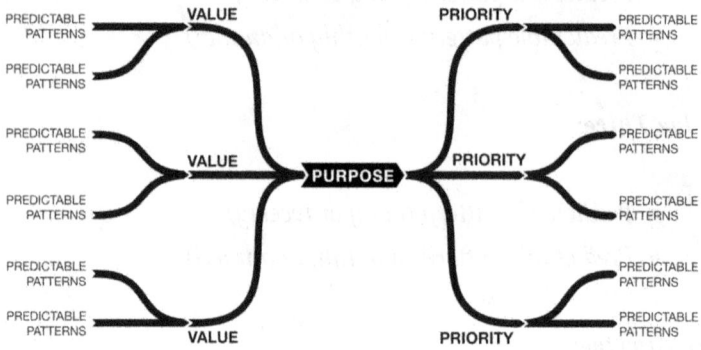

Cool huh? Now let's make it real.

11
MAKE IT REAL

Vision without execution is hallucination - Thomas Edison

There is a mantra in the startup world that goes something like this: "ship or die!" Which is just a way to remind yourself that ideas are cheap, and it's the execution of those ideas, that leads to success. That's not to say that merely executing a poor idea will get you there. What is true though, is that a decent idea executed now and with a commitment to get better incrementally over time will always be better than waiting for the idea to be perfect before moving forward. If you're waiting for the perfect idea, vision, or plan, then you will never move forward.

You now have a vision for the future of a life designed to channel your time to what matters most to you. It's time to execute!

Making room

The first step toward executing and implementing the life you have designed is to get out your time diary that represents how your time currently flows (or doesn't). Just like the architects of a river restoration project, you need to get an honest and accurate idea of what needs to be removed, what needs to stay, and what needs to be restored. Are there obstacles like social media or other time-wasters blocking the flow of your time? Commit to ripping them out of your schedule. Have obstacles and diversions overtaken helpful habits? Make a plan to restore them to your calendar. Are there things on your time diary that fit your values, purpose, and priorities? Make sure they stay.

It can be helpful to take a highlighter and highlight everything on your current schedule that seems to serve one of your values or priorities. It's worth asking if it's possible to make these things even more predictable so that they are sure to channel time consistently and reliably. It's also worth asking if these existing habits are focused enough.

It is critical to go over your time diary and highlight everything that represents someone else's purpose and priorities. Take an honest look and ask yourself what adjustments to those time commitments you can make right away? Can you make a plan to reduce the time that gets diverted away from your values, purpose, and priorities? It may not be possible to back out of everything entirely and all at once, but I'm willing to bet you can cut down on the amount of flow that those diversions get.

After you've identified what needs to go, what needs to stay, and what can be reduced, make a list of recurring time commitments that you have some ability to schedule. These are the things you have to keep doing but could do whenever it's convenient for you. Next, make a list of those recurring commitments that are absolutely out of your ability to schedule. I'm talking about things where there is genuinely no negotiating when and how often they happen.

For our family, school activities and the daily drop off and pick up schedule fell under this category. Eventually, the only thing standing between us and our dream of a season of full-time travel as a family was school. So we took our kids out of school and, for now, we let the world we encounter, and their curiosity set the curriculum. Once you start to get free a little, you want a lot. However, we started smaller and executed our design as much as we could. We started letting the current of our time flow and evolve, and we freed up more and more of our time from diversions and obstacles.

Get predictable about everything

Another way to free up more time is to get predictable about everything. Up until now, I have only suggested defining predictable patterns attached directly to your values and priorities. I'm going to go out on a limb and guess that things like "doing the laundry" or "meal planning" didn't make the list. The truth is that in our busy lives today, we tend to squeeze these sorts of tasks into the leftover margins of our schedules or try to multi-task and combine them with something else. This tendency to merely get by with the basic tasks that make life work is a significant contributing factor to how we *feel* about our time. On top of that, tackling these tasks piecemeal can often lead to spending more time on them than if we could get them done in just one predictable chunk of time. So get predictable about everything you possibly can.

Instead of doing laundry throughout the week in the little cracks of time available and feeling like the task is never done (hint: it never is), schedule a chunk of time once a week and leave it at that. Of course, there is always freedom within the framework, but I'll wager that if you give it a try and set up the predictable pattern, you will find it's possible to spend less time doing laundry.

Instead of wandering through the grocery store shopping for whatever seems good to you in the moment, schedule some time to come up with a predictable pattern of food and meals. Our family has the same seven dinners every week. I know that sounds extreme, but honestly, no one in the family minds eating our same favorite foods on a predictable rotating basis. It makes everything from shopping for food to meal prep take less time and energy. Also... freedom. If we feel like something special, we make something special. Sometimes we go out. Sometimes we end up in a location where our usual menu doesn't work, and we adapt and evolve for a season. The point is that we value our time for fun and relationships more than the time it takes to pull off a wide variety of cuisine at home. There is a lot of room here to get predictable and still have variety. Figure out what works for you. Get predictable, and you will save time and feel less busy because it's not occupying your mind continuously.

I am aware that I can quickly reach a point every day when I am feeling fatigued by the number of decisions necessary to make a life of full-time family travel work. I think most people suffer at some level from what is known as *decision fatigue*. It's real, and it reduces my capacity to accomplish much of what matters most to me. Getting predictable about all the little things helps me to avoid decision fatigue. I have had the same breakfast nearly every day for the past three years. One apple cut into 24 pieces, one banana cut into 24 pieces, and a couple of tablespoons worth of peanut butter. It works for me, and I never have to spend a single ounce of energy on deciding what to have for breakfast.

When it comes to other "start the day" decisions that I want to make predictable, I am fast moving toward what amounts to a "uniform" wardrobe. I honestly don't care about clothes and deeply resent any time lost to shopping for them. These represent choices that fit my personal values and priorities. Yours will most likely be different. My 17-year-old daughter certainly has different values when it comes to her wardrobe and as long as it all fits in her one carry-on and a small backpack (*keep it simple* is also a value for the whole family) then great!

It's worth repeating at this point, because you may not believe me, that I am naturally a spontaneous and unstructured person. However, I have discovered that embracing simple, predictable patterns around all the little things in life allows me to feel a stronger sense of freedom and creativity during my unstructured time. For example, by embracing structure around my wardrobe, I'm helping to ensure that I regularly have the time for a walk in the woods. It's merely a way of channeling more time into things I truly value.

If you think about it, these tasks feed your values and flow out of your purpose and priorities. They are the flows of time that increase our capacity and the contribution we can make to the world around us. Even the ones that don't seem to match up often are influenced by what matters to you — my value of keeping things simple influences my feelings toward both my clothing and my breakfast.

Your values and priorities will be different than mine, and so your patterns will be different. Take the time to get predictable about even the small routines of life. I promise it will help make space for what matters most to you.

Put it on your calendar

Now I want you to start scheduling your predictable patterns into your everyday life, but there's a strategy I want you to follow.

Imagine a large mason jar full to the brim with stones, tiny pebbles, and grains of sand. It's so full that the pebbles are filling in all the space between the larger stones and grains of sand are filling every tiny crack and crevice of space left over. Can you picture it? Okay, now imagine I dumped it all out and separated everything then asked you to fill it up again just like it was so that nothing is left out. What order would you start putting in the items?

If you start with the sand, I guarantee you'll run out of space for the pebbles and stones. If you start with the pebbles, you may get a little closer, but there will still be some stones left out. The only way to fit it all in and have nothing left over is to start with the larger stones. Then if you put the tiny pebbles in, they will fill in the available spaces. You may need to give it a few shakes, but with little effort, they'll find space between the stones. Then you can pour the fine grains of sand slowly into the jar and watch them easily find the space between it all.

That is how I want you to think about your schedule. I want you to think about your predictable patterns like the larger stones in the jar. They have to go on your calendar first, or all the other "stuff" of everyday life that comes up will start "filling up the jar." You'll be left with reduced capacity in your life and won't have large enough uninterrupted spaces for what's truly important. However, if you put your predictable patterns into your schedule and protect them, you'll be surprised to find that most of the everyday stuff can easily fit around them.

> *What you absolutely must not do is leave your schedule "wide open" and let other people fill it.*

Before I started making breakfast with my family a predictable pattern, I would often say yes to early morning meetings for coffee or breakfast. Those meetings weren't bad, and I still enjoy them on very rare occasions when it's the only time to schedule an important meeting. However, I decided to make breakfast with my family a predictable pattern, so I started saying I wasn't available early in the morning and suggesting an alternative time that fit in between the "large stones" which I had designed for my life. You know what? It was no big deal, and I readily found other times if it was necessary to meet with people.

So go ahead and get out a blank calendar and start scheduling your predictable patterns when they seem best to *you*. If you have some commitments that have to stay and can't be negotiated, then stick those in there and work around them. Do what you can to make the schedule *predictable*. Remember my story about the recycling pickup? If you have to check the calendar constantly because you're moving your patterns around from day to day and week to week, then you'll lose some of the value of designing your life this way.

It doesn't always have to be at the same time as long as it's easy to remember. For instance, we don't eat breakfast at the same time every day right now (though there have been seasons when that was true), but it's easy for me to remember that I'm going to do it. On the other hand, our weekly meal night happens on the same day at the same time, so it's easy for everyone to remember and make it a part of their schedule.

In fact, for years, there were around 50 people eating dinner in our home, whether we were there or not. We simply put a code lock on our door and empowered some friends to host it in our place when we needed to be out of town. That may seem extreme to you, but it was a natural outflow of our family's purpose, which is *to create space for people to gather so that relationships grow and we all become family*. No one ever had to wonder whether the meal would happen or not. Friends and neighbors could count on it, and they knew they could invite others into our predictable pattern without checking whether it was happening.

Put the big stones in the jar first. For me, these are the predictable patterns that need the most space on the calendar like our anniversary trip or our family vacation. Then move on to the large stones like your monthly predictable patterns that take up a whole (or part of a) day. Put them on the calendar first and protect them or you'll end up without large enough chunks of time and end up sacrificing the flow of life you've worked hard to design. Even if it will take you weeks (or months) to clear enough space on your calendar for your weekly predictable patterns, start putting them in the schedule where you want things to be and work toward making it a reality.

Balance the flow

Overwork, or at least an imbalance tipping toward the work side of things, seems to be an epidemic these days. We seem to spend so much of our time on work—at our jobs and when we're home—that we're always tired and depleted. Many of us reach the weekend or vacation time, and we crash—needing to recover from our work. That is not the same as rest. Crashing and recovery will never be as efficient at restoring your capacity as a balanced life designed to channel time into your values in a consistent and predictable flow.

If too little time is flowing into the rest side of your life, and too much is flowing out in the form of work, then your life is unsustainable, and you will crash. For this reason, I suggest checking the balance of your schedule once you have your predictable patterns on the calendar. I like to color-code things according to rest (capacity building) and work (capacity depleting). If an activity is both, then ask yourself which way it leans. By sorting your schedule in this way, it's easy to tell if things are out of balance. Do you have a day that is particularly heavy on the work side of things? Maybe you should make sure there's a capacity building pattern to start the next day.

I think this way of looking at balance in our designs for life is more helpful than the popular work/life spectrum. It can be impossible to separate what is work and what is life. This way of thinking discounts the fact that work is *part* of your life, and that work includes many things that don't produce income. Think of a flow system where one half collects flow capacity, and the other half gives that capacity away. That is a much more flexible and realistic way of thinking about our entire life. The good news is that by paying attention first to the rest side of the system, you will ensure that there is a sufficient and sustainable flow of time and energy for the work that matters most to you.

Remember, you cannot give away what you haven't first received.

Do The Work

To summarize, your tasks in this chapter are:

1. Analyze your time diary. Indicate recurring events and commitments that represent external values and priorities. Are there obstacles like social media or other time-wasters blocking the flow of your time? Commit to ripping them out of your schedule. Have obstacles and diversions overtaken helpful habits? Make a plan to restore them to your calendar. Are there things on your time diary that fit your values, purpose, and priorities? Make sure they stay.
2. Get out a blank calendar and start scheduling your predictable patterns when they seem best

to *you*. If you have some commitments that have to stay and can't be negotiated, then stick those in there and work around them. Do what you can to make the schedule *predictable*.
3. Take an honest look at the amounts of time devoted to capacity building values (rest) and capacity draining priorities (work). Are these amounts in balance? Consider making adjustments to your design to ensure that you have the capacity needed to accomplish your priorities in a sustainable way that leads to growth and increased capacity over time.

12

STAY FLEXIBLE

There is a saying that I believe to be true: "water finds a way." Whether it's rainwater finding the weakest link in the construction and weatherproofing of your house, or the relentless flow of water to the lowest geographical point possible, water finds a way.

I was reminded of this over the past summer when I visited Zion National Park. The main attraction of Zion is the incredibly beautiful canyon carved over millions of years by the flow of the Virgin River. There is one road that follows the river deep into the heart of the canyon. The road ends at the entrance to the iconic "Narrows" section of the river, but before you get there, you'll pass dozens of smaller streams and washes which channel water to the bottom of the canyon. Seep springs feed some of these and others only flow seasonally or when it rains.

A popular stop on the way to the narrows is the Emerald Pools. It's an easy hike up to the Lower Emerald Pools where you'll find a couple of small pools of water fed by a small creek and a dramatic waterfall. The route of that creek—carving a channel in the rock on its way to the pools and the river below—has been more or less the same for as long as Zion has been a national park. That is, it was the same until two days before I arrived with my family.

On July 11, 2018, a storm dumped a massive amount of rain in a small amount of time, and a pile of car-sized boulders came crashing down into the creek bed that feeds the lower pools. The boulders demolished the trail that leads from the lower to the upper pools completely blocking access. Eight months later, we humans have not found a way to reroute the flow of hikers safely. The water in that creek is a different story though. When I stood in the shadow of that pile of gigantic boulders two days after the storm, water had already found a way around those boulders and was flowing into the lower pools. Water finds a way.

This freedom to flow around obstacles and find new paths to maintain access to the currents of the flow system is a crucial part of nature's design, as stated by the Constructal Law. Here it is again:

> **For a finite-size flow system to persist in time (to live), its configuration must *evolve freely* in such a way that it provides greater and greater access to the currents that flow through it.**

This may seem like common sense. Of course a river will find a way to flow around a boulder. Of course a tree's root system will find a way around a buried sewer pipe. Of course natural flow systems will evolve in the face of obstacles and environmental changes to maintain and improve access to currents that flow through them. However, this is a critical point to remember as you begin to live into the flow system you have designed.

Far too often, the flow systems designed by humans lack the freedom to evolve when necessary. Airports, highway systems, and infrastructure of all sorts are plagued with designs that are rigid and can't be easily adapted if the flow of humans changes significantly over time. This fact is one of the main challenges facing the implementation of permanent mass transit infrastructure in rapidly growing cities. A light rail system is complicated to change once built. Many cities are opting for the much more adaptable solution of Bus Rapid Transit for the early stages of transit flow design because it can "evolve freely."

My point is that for this life you have designed to "persist in time," it must be allowed to evolve freely. You must be like water and find a way around the obstacles that will come your way. I have chosen my words carefully. Predictable does not mean set in stone. It's better to think of the flow system you've designed as a *flexible framework* rather than a rigid schedule. You have a structure that makes time flow predictably to the things that matter to you, but there is *freedom* within the framework.

Currently, I travel full-time with my family. We may be in the same place for a few months or only a few weeks. Every time we set up life in a new location, I find there is a unique landscape full of challenges to living out my normal predictable patterns. It can take a few days or even a week or two before things begin to flow predictably the way I've designed. This adaptation can involve changes both big and small, but the point is to stay flexible and look for the natural flow that helps my predictable patterns adapt to the unique landscape of each place and culture. You may not change locations every couple of months, but I'm sure the landscape does occasionally shift around you, and you will need to stay flexible.

Before embarking on our current season of full-time travel, our family lived in the same house near the urban core of Grand Rapids, MI. I had a lot of long-established rhythms and predictable patterns. Even there, obstacles would force me to let my patterns evolve freely. The most significant barriers were usually the terrible weather conditions that would oppress us for half the year. Winter would show up, and I'd suddenly have to find an extra hour or *five* for shoveling the driveway and sidewalks. Some weeks it didn't snow, and some weeks it snowed without end. Be like water, and find a way to flow around the obstacles that come your way.

Whether it's a unique project at work or changing market conditions, you will need to allow your predictable patterns and the flow of your values and priorities to evolve freely, or the design will be too brittle to stand the test of time. It is this freedom to evolve that gives the designs we make for our lives the same durability as rivers that flow, trees that grow, and the persistent tree-like designs we see over and over again in nature. Without the freedom to evolve, we lose the benefits of using the laws of physics, which have perfected the design of flow systems over millions of years. Without the freedom to evolve, the shape and structure of our predictable patterns over time, entropy will catch up to us, and our lives will tend toward complexity and chaos.

So yes, you will need to put energy into maintaining this flow system you have designed. We cannot escape the laws of physics. It takes effort to fend off the pull of entropy. It also takes energy to defy gravity and stand up on our own two feet. If we are able, we stand up and walk around because mobility is worth the effort. Maintaining predictable patterns that channel time and energy to the things that matter most to you is also worth it!

Use your filters

One way to stay flexible is to think of your *values* and *priorities* as filters for the everyday stuff that comes your way. You have your predictable patterns down on your calendar, and you're ready to live the life you've always wanted. What about all the time in your schedule not covered by the predictable patterns? What about all the day to day stuff that makes up your life at work and home? I'm glad you asked.

You should think of your predictable patterns as the small streams that create pathways to the more permanent tributaries (values and priorities) which eventually feed the main river (your purpose). Those small streams collect the rain that falls all around them and channel them towards the main river. Your predictable patterns are creating reliable pathways to your values and from your priorities. They are building capacity for more time to flow into values and out of your priorities.

The next step is to use your values and priorities as filters for the rest of your time. Every opportunity or request for your time needs to flow through a value or priority. If it doesn't match up, then that opportunity, activity, or request represents the values and priorities of someone else. If something doesn't match your values or priorities, be very careful about saying yes to it. It will not feed your purpose, and it's unlikely to lead to the life of your dreams.

I know there are just some things in life that we can't say no to. However, I have found that most things are negotiable when it comes to the details. Is there some way of changing the details that make it a better fit with your values and priorities? Is there any room for negotiation? Give it a try, because the world needs what you will contribute when you're free to live your purpose with as much of your capacity as you can throw at it.

War-time rhythms

One last thought about staying flexible.

Sometimes, life gets crazy. Sometimes it's by choice, and sometimes the storms just come your way. You need a plan to deal with those times when they arrive. Maybe you've decided to tackle a hard project in a relatively short amount of time, and that means chucking the regular, predictable schedule out the window. Maybe you're moving, and you need to drop everything for weeks to pack up the house and prepare for it. Perhaps it's a job loss or a personal tragedy. Maybe it's a season of intensive training.

There are plenty of circumstances that could cause you to have to sweep normal life to the side and devote significant amounts of time and energy to something temporary and all-consuming. I refer to times like this as "war-time."

For the United States, World War II was all-consuming from an economic and resource perspective. The government found it necessary to ration food, gas and even clothing because so much of the country's resources were flowing into the war effort. Americans were asked to conserve everything no matter if it was officially rationed or not. The rhythms of everyday life were changed dramatically. People made sacrifices because they knew it was important and that it was temporary.

There will be times when you need to shift into dramatically different rhythms and patterns to deal with what comes your way. At times it may be the only way to achieve an important goal. When these times come along and force you into "war-time" rhythms, remember two things.

First, remember that these times are temporary. Even if it feels like the situation won't end, don't let the extraordinary circumstances lead to a set of rhythms that become normal life. Make a plan to transition back to the rhythms of life that you have designed. Your design may need to evolve as a result of your extraordinary experience but do not let the pace of life required by that experience endure long after it's over. World War II ended, and the rationing of resources ended with it. The experience changed the country, but some version of normal life resumed in the post-war years. Remember, this too shall pass.

Second, don't throw all rhythms of life out in the face of difficulty or exceptional circumstances. Take a step back and ask yourself what predictable patterns you can keep or adjust during "war-time." This perspective is especially important for patterns on the rest side of the system that flow into your values. Without any rhythms, even if they are the bare essentials, you are likely to end up with diminished capacity and risk becoming just a dry riverbed with little to no available energy. Think of this as rationing. What rhythms and predictable patterns can you implement to make sure you have the capacity you need to make it through the storm.

The past three months have been a little bit of a war-time season for me. Writing doesn't come easily for me, but this book has been a long-time goal. I decided to take these three months and treat writing the first draft of this book as my full-time job. That meant I had to dramatically change my everyday rhythms and cut back my other priorities to the bare minimum to have enough capacity to accomplish this goal. I don't think that I would have been able to work on it a few hours per week for months and months until it was done. Writing doesn't flow like that for me. It felt more like I needed to attack the goal with the blunt force of concentrated effort. It's been a rewarding challenge.

For me, this project has mostly meant changes to the predictable patterns on the work side of my life with a few tweaks on the rest side. Because I was able to choose this project and make a plan for it, the result is not so dramatic. However, I made a plan to transition back to my normal rhythms and patterns of flow when this project was over.

Don't wait until extraordinary circumstances have drained all of your capacity away, before taking a small step back and making a plan to get through the challenge and maybe even grow stronger along the way.

Do The Work

This chapter is mostly about changing your mindset from thinking about your schedule as less of a rigid routine to more of a flexible framework. However, to help you prepare for the obstacles and war-times when they come, take some time to **consider and write down those predictable patterns that should be on the "ration list."**

Which habits need to be kept in some shape or form even when the storms of life rage? If you have an idea about what these are, it will make it easier to transition to war-time rhythms when necessary.

13

BEWARE THE ARROW OF TIME

Here in the last chapter before the epilogue of this book, I want to leave you with a little extra motivation. I know that following through with the concepts in this book is no easy task. I know this because the laws of physics say that the path of least resistance is the one that leads toward disorder, complexity, and chaos. The laws of physics say that designing and implementing structure and simplicity in your life requires extra effort. Do you remember why?

I introduced these concepts along with the 2nd Law of Thermodynamics and entropy in chapter three. I want to return to these concepts of physics and take a look at one more principle that is directly related to the increasing entropy of our universe, the *arrow of time*.

Let me start by clarifying what physicists mean when they say *spacetime*. Everyone is familiar with the three dimensions of space. They are the three dimensions that make a ball different from a two-dimensional circle. They are what we mean when we say something is in 3D. Ever since Albert Einstein and the Theory of General Relativity, a 4th dimension has been added into the mix. Now *time* is considered a dimension of our universe and that's why we say "spacetime" when we're talking about the physics of the universe.

We usually talk about the three dimensions of space as a set of three axes labeled X, Y, and Z. We illustrate these axes as three intersecting lines with arrows pointing in all directions. The arrows on both ends of these lines have significance. They represent the fact that there is no directional *preference* when it comes to the three dimensions of space.

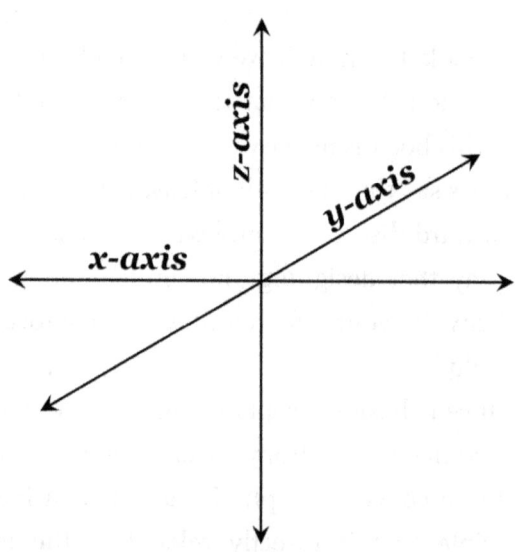

We can imagine objects being moved in any direction in space with ease. Time is different. Time is drawn as a line with only *one* arrow on its end. Time is the one dimension with an asymmetrical directional preference. In other words, time only moves in one direction. This concept is what physicists call, **the arrow of time.**

The Arrow Of Time →

It may seem like just common sense and not at all surprising to you since this is how we experience time every moment of every day. The past is different from the present, is different from the future. Time passes moment by moment and we cannot easily undo the effects of time passing. For example, if an egg falls off of the counter and breaks on the floor, we can't reverse time and unbreak that egg. The other three dimensions are different, though. Imagine instead of an egg; a ball falls onto the floor. We could easily pick the ball up and put it back on the counter. The ball is back where it started, but we can't erase the fact that it did fall off the counter and onto the floor. Time only moves in one direction. No surprise, right?

It is surprising from a physics perspective though. The fact that this one dimension only moves forward and never backward demands some sort of explanation. As it turns out, I've already covered the reason, but I've been saving time's arrow until the end. Time has an arrow because entropy is increasing in our universe. Remember the 2nd Law of thermodynamics? Entropy increases. That's what makes today different from yesterday. It is why we experience time as a relentless march forward second by second, minute by minute, and year by year. It's why we know things with clarity about the past but not about the future.

No Do-overs

The arrow of time is why the past is unchangeable but the future is not. In other words, there are no do-overs. You can't choose to have had something different for dinner yesterday, but you can choose what to have for dinner tonight. It may seem like I'm being Captain Obvious here, but I find that I often behave as if this isn't the case. I know I'm not the only one. I often waste time as if it's a renewable resource, but it isn't. We can't go back and make different choices about time that has past.

I don't mean to be obnoxious, but I'm not sure this reality always sinks in. We put off making changes and procrastinate pursuing our dreams. There's plenty of time for all of that later, we say. Is there really though?

The truth is, this way of thinking about time as something we can "save" for the future is tied to our culture's extremely unhelpful obsession with equating time and money. It's then exacerbated by focusing most of our "work" or productive time on things that generate financial capital. Time and money are not the same, and don't behave the same way at all in our lives.

Money is more like the ball that falls off the counter. You can do all sorts of interesting things with it if you have the right perspective about it's value. You can spend it. You can lend it out and watch it do some good and come back to you with the same fundamental value. You can invest it and watch it grow and come back to you with an increase in value. We can be very intentional about how we use money right now or we can save it for the future where it retains or even increases in value.

Time doesn't work this way. Time is more like the egg that falls off the counter. Once it happens, there's no going back. We can't really lend time to someone else to increase their own available time. We can't really invest it in order to seek a return of more time than someone else. Time is spent and it passes whether we are intentional about it or not. Once it passes it is gone. You cannot save time for later.

And since we may eventually retire from the income-generating part of our "work," we don't want to stop offering the meaningful result of living out our purpose in the world. That leads to an unfulfilled and unhappy life. While there may be very good reasons to delay gratification when it comes to financial capital, there is every reason to not delay gratification when it comes to how you use your time.

Many of us spend our time in the present as if it's gaining us time in the future, as if we could trade time while we're young and our kids are around, for money and security and a similar quality and quantity of time later. We can't. Entropy and the Arrow Of Time ensure that the time we spend now is gone, while we and everyone around us relentlessly grow older (gain entropy). Bummer, I know.

So many of us abuse our values and the capacity of our bodies now in the present, making a futile attempt to gain freedom later. Leisure is not the same as freedom. Now is the time to pursue your purpose and live the life of your dreams. It takes work to overcome the increasing entropy of the universe, but it is possible. The world around us is full of beautiful examples of life and movement pushing back against the relentless force of entropy and time. Learn from the rivers and the trees. Look to the design of your own body and design the flow of your time.

You can't change the past, but you can choose right now to change the future. Make the effort to design the flow of time in your life toward what matters most to you, then put that design into practice. Declare your purpose and make a stand for your values and priorities. Live the rest of your life full of purpose, on purpose.

Don't waste time on regret.

You can't change the past. It's science!

You *can* change the future and everything else about your circumstances. It's hard work, but the results are worth it.

Go change your life! You got this!

EPILOGUE

Change is hard. Coaching is the answer.

I've read countless books about how to change my life, improve my skills as a leader, or how to be a better parent. I've been to dozens of conferences, summits, and seminars to try to make progress towards the big goals I've had in life. I've watched TED talk after TED talk until I was so inspired I thought I might burst. I tend to be an information junkie so, to be honest, I love all these things. They make me feel like I'm better somehow or smarter than I was before. Every little bit helps, right?

The hard truth of the matter is that none of those things led to much change in my everyday habits and routines. You know, those day to day predictable patterns that represent the flow system of our lives? They're almost entirely unaffected by the books I've read, the videos I've watched, or the inspiring talks I heard at conferences.

However, over the last decade, I have changed the day to

day design of my life which enabled me to reach many of the big goals I set for myself. So, how did I do it? What works?

First, It helps to speak your goals out loud. Share them with your friends. Share them with your partners in life. I used this practice as I was writing this book, and it was a huge help. I told everyone I met that I was going to dedicate three straight months to get my thoughts down in the shape of this book. There were plenty of days during those three months that I did not feel like writing, but the idea of so many people knowing my goal helped to motivate me to keep up with the predictable patterns I set to meet my goal. I didn't want to have to explain why I didn't do what I said I would do.

This strategy tends to work best for short term goals. If your goal is something that will take a long time to accomplish or if the change requires a considerable investment of time that you don't currently have, then you may be setting yourself up to fail. Just speaking your goals out loud will only take you so far.

Second, it can be a huge help to find someone who has done something similar to what you wish to accomplish and ask them to mentor you along the way. If you have a big goal that will take a long time to accomplish, it will be invaluable to have access to someone who has already made the journey.

As I've mentioned, my family and I are currently traveling full time. Living this way is incredibly rewarding, but it is also a massive shift from what we were used to. We read as many books and blogs as we could find before we decided to take the plunge, but we also reached out to a few families who have been traveling for years now and asked them to help us make the transition. Talking to those families and being able to ask them questions along the way has been far more helpful than anything we read. We consider those families to be our mentors, and they've also become some of our closest friends. Don't be afraid to ask someone you respect for a little help. In my experience, people are usually flattered to be asked and more than willing to provide any support they can.

Lastly, there are some things in life that we will struggle to accomplish without the help and guidance of a good coach. This truth is something that high-performance athletes, business executives, and elite entrepreneurs know already. It's time that the rest of us stop struggling to accomplish our most significant goals on our own. A good coach will bring focus to your goals and help you design a path to reach your vision for the future. They will be there to help you prune out whatever is blocking that path. They'll help you grow your capacity until the seemingly impossible becomes a reality. They'll keep you accountable for progress along the way.

No one outside of my family had a more significant impact on me as a teenager than my wrestling coach. No one. He was my biggest cheerleader on and off the mat. He was there when I was making mistakes to help me correct my course (mostly off the mat). He was there to tell me my dreams weren't big enough and to push me further than I thought possible. He was there to help me bring discipline to my training and to teach me new skills that would take advantage of my specific mix of strengths. I had many teachers who managed to make an impression on me, but nothing came close to the impact left by my coach.

Much later on in life when I was struggling to make progress on the important goals I longed to accomplish, I hired a coach to help. I made more progress in a year than in the previous five. I was able to make hard changes and make them stick. Looking back, it should be no surprise, but at the time, it was. I resisted the investment of financial capital because money seemed so precious and finite. The return on that investment has been immense and not just financially. I've had a few coaches since then, and they've helped me level up in every area of my life. I've gained knowledge and wisdom. I've gained freedom over my time and built stronger relationships. All of which is worth far more to me than the financial capital, I invested in making those gains in my life.

Today I spend much of my time coaching others. However, I still invest time and treasure to have a coach help me set goals and make progress towards them week in and week out.

If you want to make lasting changes to your life and reach the goals that seem persistently out of reach, then I encourage you to find a coach to help you. Coaching works, it's as simple as that. It works for a high school wrestling team, and it works for Fortune 500 CEOs. It will work for you.

If you have questions about coaching or anything in this book, don't hesitate to send me an email at **andy@andy-dragt.com**

You can find out more about me and the coaching I do at **andydragt.com**

I am rooting for you to get free and build the life of your dreams!

ACKNOWLEDGMENTS

No creative work happens in a vacuum. This book would not exist without the support of family, mentors, teachers, and other authors who make the mysteries of science approachable to mere mortals. I hope these pages make them proud and count as some small reward for the contribution each of them has made not only to this project but my life as a whole.

Specifically, I would like to thank:

First and foremost, my partner in everything, Gina. Everything good or useful about the content of this book begins with her. She is the very genesis of structure in my life. She helped me to overcome the chaos I had created on my own. Her support and belief inspired me to give shape and structure to these ideas in this form. Always the first to read. Always the first to edit. Always the first to cheer me on. It is not an overstatement to say that there would be no book without her. I'm thankful for all the ways that she has transformed my life through her patient love and support!

I had many early readers who offered feedback and encouragement along the way. I'm grateful for each one, but two stand out in particular. Azizi Birkeland was the first to annotate an early draft thoroughly, and the book is better because of her feedback. Brandon Pearce was the first to read and work through all the content with fresh eyes. I'm grateful to them both for their support, feedback, and encouragement.

Speaking of feedback, I used The Spun Yarn (thespunyarn.com) to get quality and unbiased feedback from trusted readers on an early draft of this book. The value of their service blew me away. I can't recommend them highly enough. Thank you to Sarah Beaudette and my Spun Yarn Readers!

A special thanks to my launch team for helping me lift this material out of the depths of obscurity faced by a first-time author: Linnea Carlson deRoche, Steven Depolo, Sherry Gant, Brandon Pearce, Haeli Dragt, Maya Dragt, Brandon Lemberg, Joris Hoogendoorn, Erica VanEe, Jennifer Dragt, Dave DeJonge, Jim Davis, Anna Leitch, Kris Garapati, and Sharon Wheeler.

I am grateful to Adrian Bejan not only for his work to uncover and define the Constructal Law but also for his ability to explain it in a way that can be understood by the likes of me. I have read and attempted to understand many technical books on various topics within the field of physics. Most are a bit like being stuck in the morning fog; if you stick it out and give it time, the fog lifts and you gain clarity on the subject matter. Adrian Bejan has a knack for writing in a way that is accessible to the masses, and it's like taking in a view of the Grand Canyon on a bright sunny day. I have found his body of work to be of immense value and I'm grateful for his labor. If you're interested in a more in-depth look at the Constructal Law, I suggest starting with *Design In Nature*.

I am similarly in debt to Simon Sinek and his team for how I think about the topic of purpose. After many years of digesting nearly everything I could find on purpose, vision, and direction for life, I (like countless others) happened upon Simon's TED talk. The rest is history. His work has so utterly shaped my thoughts and methods of coaching that I can't tell where his body of work ends, and my own ideas and innovations begin. While this book includes a healthy section on purpose, it's not intended to be the sole focus. For further help and guidance on this crucial piece of the overall puzzle that is a well-designed life, I highly recommend *Start With Why* and *Finding Your Why* as the place to start.

Finally, I want to thank my girls, Haeli and Maya—for their constant love, understanding, and support! Every day of my life, I hear that I'm the best daddy ever and about their belief that I can do anything. It may not be precisely accurate, but their faith in me leads to an unreasonable amount of courage to tackle hard things. They always stand up for what's right and never accept the status quo. I am more proud of them than I could ever adequately express.

Thank you all,

Andy

ABOUT THE AUTHOR

Andy Dragt was born and raised in Michigan, USA. He is an author, speaker, and coach passionately leading the way toward healthy balanced lives and stronger family relationships. He is a certified executive leadership coach and has worked with hundreds of people all over the world to design and live a prioritized life at work and home. UNBUSY is the result of countless hours of coaching and conversations around the biggest obstacle for many to living out their purpose and dreams for life.

Andy is also the co-founder of Global Families, a network for families who travel and travelers in search of a family. After years of creating space for families to gather in their Michigan home, the Dragt family decided to create a welcoming space online. Families can discover together the most inspiring ways to develop deep and meaningful connections and the path to more intentional living and learning through travel. Find out more at globalfamilies.net.

Since 2017, Andy and his family have been charting an intentional path of worldwide travel. They desire to learn all they can from the people and cultures they encounter and be transformed by the experience along the way. This hands-on and experiential learning as a family has been their dream for quite some time and was made possible by the tools and concepts in this book.

Andy is available for select speaking engagements. To inquire about a possible appearance, please send a note to andy@andydragt.com or visit andydragt.com.

www.ingramcontent.com/pod-product-compliance
Lightning Source LLC
Chambersburg PA
CBHW070153100426
42743CB00013B/2899